Fostering Innovation

Fostering Innovation

How to Build an Amazing IT Team

Andrew Laudato

WILEY

This book is dedicated to CIOs. Long underappreciated, disrespected, and misunderstood, they are now at the center of our digital world.

About the Author

Andrew Laudato started his career as a computer programmer and quickly realized he was as passionate about business as he is about technology. The intersection of business and technology is where innovation happens and where people and companies succeed.

After spending more than 20 years as a CIO/CTO, Laudato currently serves as the executive vice president and chief operating officer of The Vitamin Shoppe. In this role, he leads operations across digital commerce, information technology, enterprise portfolio management, supply chain, strategic sourcing, and commercialization.

Laudato is a member of the CNBC technology executive council and the New York City CIO executive council and is a founding member of George Mason University's Center for Retail Transformation. In addition, he serves on the board of Lideranca, a private company focused on diversity, equity, and inclusion.

Learn more at andrewlaudato.com.

About the Technical Proofreader

Kristian Kimbro Rickard is the founder and CEO of Doyenne360, a social-impact technology company. With a track record for designing, building, and rapidly deploying AI, analytics, and workforce collaboration and training solutions, Doyenne360, and its AI-powered STEM workforce development platform called STEMNXT, serve organizations in industries such as education, oil and gas, and retail.

Kristian has more than two decades of experience in technology, starting her career after graduating from Texas Tech University with a Master's in Technical Communication, specializing in online design and development. Beginning as a software developer at a Big Five management consulting firm, she advanced into technical leadership roles in consulting, spent five years at Microsoft headquarters honing her business, finance, and product management skills to add to her technical expertise portfolio, and launched her first startup, MAX451, in 2011.

Kristian has received numerous accolades as a technologist and an entrepreneur: she has been listed as one of the top ten female entrepreneurs to watch by the Global Accelerator Network (GAN), and her work has been featured in a variety of publications, including CIO Magazine, Retail TouchPoints, Information Week, and Microsoft advanced analytics customer case studies.

Kristian enjoys traveling internationally to speak about technology and the importance of increasing diversity and inclusion within the technology field. Passionate about seeing more women and people of color in technical leadership roles, you can often find Kristian in schools within her community, volunteering her time to teach middle and high-school students how to assemble robots, how to code, or how to make a flashing dance-party bracelet with some duct tape, LED lights, and a little knowledge about how to create circuits.

Acknowledgments

On May 1, 2018, I was in the audience at an industry conference, and it occurred to me that I should write a book. I sent a note to my partner, Kristian Kimbro Rickard, asking her thoughts. Her response, which I still have, was an enthusiastic "Yes, yes, yes, do it, do it!" Soon after, I mentioned the idea to my daughter, Autumn Laudato, who was beyond supportive. Autumn always supports me and my endeavors, no matter how crazy they are. Autumn declared, "I'll buy the first copy!"

Although I had support, encouragement, and even a sale from the most important people in my life, I didn't do anything about it. A year later, in the summer of 2019, I mentioned the idea to my close friends Dan and Bette Apitz. A few days later, three books showed up at my door: books on writing and becoming an author. Dan and Bette didn't just give me platitudes, they decided to hold me accountable for writing this book. Each time we talked, they expected an update. There was no turning back now—Dan and Bette were not going to let that happen. This is what we all want from our friends!

As this book went from a thought, to a few notes, to an outline, and finally to words on a page, I shared drafts, ideas, and chapters with my friends for their advice. This book has been shaped, improved, and corrected by many people. Thank you to Vicki Cantrell, Paul Demboski, Chris Fadrowski, Cathy Hotka, David Kastin, Cindy Lu, Cindy Osmani, Hank Reimer, Stacey Renfro, Deanna Steel, Sheri Strobel, Lou Sterzenbach, and many others.

I've had help and support and the opportunity to work with so many talented people that I could fill another book with their names. If you feel as though you should have received a mention here, let me know, and I'll give you top billing in my next book.

I want to give special thanks to my mentors: Les Duncan, Cary Turner, Greg Rake, Alex Smith, and Sharon Leite. I've learned, and am still learning, a tremendous amount from each of you. Sharon, it's a true honor to work with you at The Vitamin Shoppe, and I am beyond grateful for the opportunities you have given and continue to give me.

I also need to acknowledge people who are no longer with us, who have meant a great deal to me: my parents, Joe and Toni Laudato; my grandmother, Lena Laudato, who told me that every time I got a raise,

I should keep my lifestyle the same and add to my savings (oh, how I wished I had listened to her advice); and Marvin Girouard, who gave me my first CIO role, before I was ready, with the directive, "Don't do anything but learn for your first year." That's a gift no first-time CIO would receive today.

An acknowledgement shout-out to the authors who took the time to speak with me as I was learning the process of writing and publishing a book. Every book takes its own path, and their insights were golden. Thank you Steve Dennis, Kris Kelso, Ron Thurston, Howard Tiersky, and Sherry Winn.

I wish to thank my agent, Jeffrey Herman, who believed in the book from the start. Thank you also to the people I worked with at Wiley: Devon Lewis, Christine O'Connor, Saravanan Dakshinamurthy, and Kelly Talbot. Devon and Christine patiently answered my questions; and yes, when I'm asking them, there is a such thing as a dumb question. Kelly, who edited my book, has the title Editor, but a better description for him would be magician. Like the grandmother who tells you that your zipper is down, Kelly gave honest, straightforward feedback.

I come from a close family, and they mean everything to me. The biggest thanks go to them. In addition to Kristian and Autumn, I'd like to thank my sisters, Renee Petro and Tina Laudato; my brother-in-law, Samir Petro; my niece and nephew, Nina and Joey Petro; my daughter-in-law, Lauren Laudato; and the woman I'm lucky enough to be able to refer to as Mom, Karen Kimbro.

And finally, thank you to my readers. I hope you find this book worthwhile and that we can continue to learn from one another.

Contents at a Glance

Contents

Introduction

Are you a CIO? Then let's face it, nobody likes you. Not your team, not your boss, not your vendor partners, and, unfortunately, not your company's functional leaders. Because of the long hours you work, your family may not be too happy with you right now, and even your dog wonders where you've been all day.

How is that possible? You work around the clock; you are constantly juggling priorities and pulling off the impossible. You and your team have saved your company from disaster on more than one occasion.

IT leaders face many challenges. The first one is that IT can do more harm than good. When everything works perfectly, success is attributed to the functional leader. High sales result from desirable products and on-point marketing. When things go wrong, there's a good chance IT will take the blame. When the network is down, the registers aren't ringing, and the website is inaccessible, sales are impacted. When projects fail to deliver the expected value—IT again becomes the scapegoat.

Another challenge IT leaders face is that we accomplish only a small fraction of what is desired. How many initiatives did your team complete last year? How many were requested? The gap is usually large. It's easy to dream up an extra feature, capability, or report. But it takes time, effort, and money to deliver those things.

Another risk for IT leaders occurs when we don't understand or relate to our business. When we become enamored with solutions, we turn into hammers looking for nails. Trying to solve a technology problem with *business* is not the path to CIO stardom.

The good news is that there has never been a better time to be an IT leader. The world is on the fast track to *digital everything,* and technology is at the center of everything we do. I bet you bought this book on a computer. You may even be reading it on one. Not that long ago, we had to go to a bookstore to buy a book. As technologists drive this transformation, our standing as leaders and innovators will continue to improve. IT leaders' opportunities for career growth have never been better. More and more, IT leaders are part of the executive committee, and they have a seat at the executive table. IT leaders are being promoted to Chief Operating Officers (COO) and Chief Executive Officers (CEO). IT leaders are being tapped for corporate board seats, as the importance of technology has expanded in every type of business, big and small.

In this book, we explore several tools and techniques for improving the IT function in your business.

Why Did I Write This Book?

My grandmother had a saying: "If not me, then whom?" Like your grandmother, she'd be the one willing to tell you that your zipper was down, your breath smelled bad, or that dress did indeed make you look fat. She'd tell the hard truth because who else would?

Let's face it: IT does not have the best reputation. We've come a long way since Nicholas Carr published "IT Doesn't Matter" in the *Harvard Business Review* in 2003, but we still have a long way to go. In many companies, IT bashing and IT scapegoating continue to be an acceptable part of the corporate culture.

If you're a struggling CIO, I hope this book will help you turn things around. If you're a new CIO, you need to learn quickly because, in the digital age, you won't have the runway that my generation did. If you're an aspiring CIO, don't let this introduction discourage you. Consider this book proof that there's a robust community of CIOs and IT leaders willing to exchange ideas and share lessons learned as you walk this path. CIO should no longer stand for *Career Is Over*. We're in the digital age, and the IT department can be an organization's most important asset.

About This Book

In this book, I provide detailed and prescriptive advice on how to best run an IT department. I do so with the understanding that there's more than one way to accomplish that goal. Your approach should vary based on the company's size, the company's plans, the CEO's style, and the team's strength. External factors, including the economy, the state of the market, customer demand, and advancements in technology all impact how you should lead.

Staying true to your values and beliefs is vital to being an open and honest leader. Don't read this book and then walk into the office on Monday morning a *new and improved you*. Continuous improvement concepts apply to our personal development as much as they do to our teams.

If your goal is to transform IT by pivoting to Agile and DevOps, you need to understand where your company is on its journey and adapt accordingly. IT leaders need to be *agile* with a little "a" before they can be *Agile* with a big "A." You will find the Agile and Lean principles woven throughout the text. Although I am a staunch Agile advocate, this is not an Agile book.

People who know me well will be shocked to see that the word *project* appears in this book over 100 times. Like George Carlin's *seven words you can't say on television*, I have a list of words I dislike. These, in no particular order, are *project*, *user*, *phase*, and *resource*. My dislike for the word *project* came from my adoption of Agile and its association with Waterfall project management. However, I'm okay with the classic definition of a project: *an activity with a defined start and stop.* We all set out to do work, and hopefully, that work gets finished in the best way possible.

I wrote this book in plain language, making it accessible and hopefully enjoyable for non-technical readers. This book will provide insights for anyone in an IT leadership role and anyone who works closely with IT leaders. In today's digital age, that's just about everyone.

Reader Support for This Book

How to Contact the Publisher

If you believe you've found a mistake in this book, please bring it to our attention. At John Wiley & Sons, we understand how important it is to provide our customers with accurate content, but even with our best efforts an error may occur.

In order to submit your possible errata, please email it to our Customer Service Team at wileysupport@wiley.com with the subject line "Possible Book Errata Submission."

Become an Empathetic Leader

1

Hey, What Do You Know?

When I got my first chief information officer (CIO) gig in August 2000, I had no clue what I was doing. The skills needed to get the job—charm and charisma—differed from the skills required to do the job.

Over the past 20-plus years as CIO, chief technology officer (CTO), and now chief operation officer (COO), I have learned many lessons, practices, and techniques that I have used to foster and develop three winning IT Departments. Most of these lessons didn't come easy; several came through failure, embarrassment, and trial and error.

We all know you learn terrific lessons from failure. You need to learn from your wins as well. What worked? Why did it work? Maybe you got lucky by hiring a hotshot project manager who muscled your initiative across the finish line. Perhaps you think you're winning, but you're destroying your team morale. Don't let the failure discourage you, and don't let the wins make you cocky. Remove emotions from your performance self-assessment. This isn't personal; it's business. You are not defined by your last project.

Build Your Skillset

An essential parenting skill is to remember when you were your kid's age. As much as the world has changed, remembering what you did, thought, and felt in middle school and high school will make you a more empathetic parent. This concept applies directly to leadership. I started as a programmer/analyst, an old term for developer. I moved my way up to senior programmer analyst, manager, senior manager, director, and then VP of applications. In each of those roles, I paid close attention to my leaders and, frankly, judged their behavior. There were some behaviors I despised, some I loved, and some I didn't understand.

By remembering what it's like to be in the trenches, you'll hopefully be a better General to your troops.

If you didn't work your way up to CIO and instead came through a different path, there's still hope for you. If your path was a boarding school, Harvard, McKinsey, and now CIO (congrats, that's impressive), you must put in extra time and energy to get honest input from the rank and file. If your path to CIO was from a business function, read *The Adventures of an IT Leader* by Robert D. Austin.[1] In that book, a functional leader complains so much about IT that the CEO puts him in charge of it. There are a lot of good insights in that book. The most important insight is understanding why the prior CIO got fired.

Technology is one part of the CIO role—albeit a small part. Five critical skills are needed to be a successful CIO:

1. People skills
2. Business expertise
3. Technical prowess
4. Project management
5. Administration

You're probably good at three or more of these, or you wouldn't have gotten the job. What's your weakest subject? Focus on rounding out your skillset in each of the areas. Put the most effort into the items you struggle with.

Grow Through Listening

As you look to improve, start by listening. Listen to your team. Listen to your peers. Seek out and listen to other CIOs. Read everything you can get your hands on. Build a network of IT leaders across your industry. Being a CIO is a lonely job. Although I use the word *peers* to describe the other executives in your company, they aren't peers in the sense that they can relate to your challenges. The first time I sat down and had a beer with a CIO from a similar-sized company in the same industry, I could feel the stress leave my body. I was not alone—CIOs in other companies have similar challenges. When I left retail and took a CIO role in senior living, the issues were remarkably similar.

Every company has challenges, and every CIO is struggling to balance the demands being placed on them. Seeking these conversations is not just imperative for your education; it's also good for your mental state.

I vividly remember an uncomfortable discussion with the chief supply chain officer. Let's call him Joe. Joe said to me, "Every day, we complete all of our work before we go home. If we get 10,000 orders, we stay until 10,000 orders are shipped. If we get 15,000 orders, then we work until they get shipped. IT only completes a small fraction of what I need. Imagine if we only shipped 100 orders and called it a day." An IT Department's unique challenge is that only a tiny percentage of what is requested ever gets completed. Keeping your business partners satisfied while rarely giving them what they want is a tricky business.

A Proactive Mindset

In January 2020, mere weeks before the coronavirus pandemic utterly disrupted our world, I was promoted from CTO to COO of The Vitamin Shoppe. While I still oversee the IT Department, I am now one of its biggest customers. We're in the digital age, and all of my functions rely heavily on technology to be successful. Seeing IT from the outside changed my perspective.

As the COO, I consider every problem in our business to be my problem. When you accept that everything is your problem, you save a lot of time and energy not being defensive and pointing fingers. Can you develop this mindset without being a COO? A leader who focuses on fixing problems is a valuable asset to their organization.

We are in a changing field in changing times. A career in technology is a lifelong commitment to learning. Having the mindset and willingness to learn and adapt is vital to building and running a world-class IT Department. In the next chapter, we'll look at what sets an IT Department head and shoulders above the rest.

2

An Amazing IT Department? What's That?

Stacey Renfro, the award-winning CEO of mDesign Home Décor, understands the importance of a strong IT Department to any business's success—especially a digital-first company. Here is Stacey's advice to CIOs:

1. Speak our language, not yours. We don't need to know how you do your work.
2. Know the business. Don't sit behind your computer and expect to make a difference.
3. Communicate. Let your business partners know what you're doing. If you don't share, you may not know all the impacts of a change.

Amazing IT Departments are a competitive advantage for their company. Amazing IT Departments continually exceed expectations by providing reliable and secure systems. They have friendly, prompt, and competent support teams. Amazing IT Departments complete their projects on time, on budget, and with a high degree of customer satisfaction. Amazing IT Departments are agile, working in small iterations and adapting on the fly. Amazing IT Departments write things down and keep good records without being buried by needless paperwork and bureaucracy. Amazing IT Departments provide transparency by communicating status, honestly, and in plain language. Amazing IT Departments are a terrific value, providing cost-effective services while delivering high return-on-investment (ROI) capabilities. Amazing IT Departments openly learn from their mistakes and successes, taking the time to look back on every initiative. Amazing IT Departments provide a fertile ground for innovation. They build flexible platforms, which allow for rapid prototyping. They have a culture that allows for innovation, and they inspire and reward creativity.

If you work in an Amazing IT Department, your work is aligned with the company's goals. You know you are making a difference. You also understand what you need to do to be successful. You have a clearly defined career path based on your personal goals. The work is rewarding because people are supportive and collaborative, and everyone on the team is pulling their weight. You can't imagine working anywhere else, and when the phone rings, you tell the recruiter you have no interest in exploring other opportunities.

Attributes of an Amazing IT Department

- Helps the company accomplish its goals
- Drives and inspires innovation
- Is an enabler, not a blocker
- Delivers cost-effective results
- Provides career growth opportunities for the team
- Is a fun and rewarding place to work

For the most part, these qualities are all attainable, although some require more awareness and commitment than others. In the next chapter, we'll examine some of the common problems that make it more difficult to build and sustain such a team.

3

Conventional Wisdom Is Wrong

If you're a sitting CIO right now, how are you doing? Use Table 3.1 to assess yourself. Answer honestly; nobody's looking. By the way, you can write in this book. You bought it.

Table 3.1: CIO Self-Assessment

Question	Yes/No/ Don't know
Are your systems reliable, with 99.9% uptime?	
Do you score over 90% on an internal customer satisfaction survey?	
Does your board of directors (board) consider IT a competitive advantage?	
Does IT provide value, continually delivering new capabilities?	
Do the CEO and CFO brag about IT in public presentations?	
Are you providing cost-effective services?	
Are you invited to informal executive conversations because the CEO values your input?	
Do your company employees find it easy to use their tools to get work done? Are their files in the cloud and easily accessible?	
Do other department heads treat you as an equal?	
Is IT turnover lower than the company average?	
Is your team fully engaged? Do they over-deliver?	
If I asked everyone on your team to list the top three IT priorities, would they all give the same answers?	
If I asked all the VPs in your company to list the top three IT priorities, would they all give the same answers?	
Is IT leading the way on innovation in your company?	

If you answered yes to most of these questions, call me—I'd like to feature you in my next book. The rest of us have some work to do.

Compared to our executive peers, our profession is still in its infancy and only recently gaining respectability. Two of the first people to have the CIO title were Al Zipf of Bank of America, and Max Hopper of Bank of America and American Airlines. "Management's Newest Star: Meet the Chief Information Officer," declared *Business Week* magazine in a headline in 1986[2]. Just 17 years later, *The Harvard Business Review* declared the profession dead, in the article "IT Doesn't Matter."[3]

Showing our worth has been a tough sell. We don't bring in revenue, mistakes can be extremely harmful, and what we do seems to take forever. Have you ever taken an introductory programming class, and the goal at the end is to get the words "Hello World" to pop up on the screen? The amount of effort necessary to make this happen is incomprehensible to our non-technical peers. One of the biggest challenges is that what we do is esoteric and more challenging than it looks.

A Tale of Two Projects

Imagine the case where a company is doing well, so it adds hundreds of people to its staff. The company's growth has created two problems: it needs a more robust people-management solution, and it needs additional parking. The decision is made to build a parking garage and implement new cloud-based human resources (HR) software. Both projects coincidentally cost around $3 million to complete.

The company performs a rigorous ROI process before software projects are approved. The chief people officer (CPO) is adamant that she needs tools for talent acquisition, compensation management, payroll, and employee development. As we know, it's hard to associate a revenue increase with this software. Costs will go up compared to their current business processes using spreadsheets and email as their primary tools. The parking garage doesn't go through the ROI process. Nobody likes to park a mile away and ride a shuttle bus back and forth. It's clearly needed.

The CFO wants estimates. The parking garage estimate is detailed and easy to understand. It includes tangible tasks such as excavation, framing, concrete, and painting. The HR project documentation is riddled with obscure jargon. The CIO is reluctant to give an estimate or a completion date for the HR project, stating that he doesn't even know what the requirements are yet.

The decision is made to complete both the parking garage and the HR software projects. Both projects complete on the same day.

There is a ribbon-cutting for the parking garage, and the employees are thrilled. No training is required since they all know how to park.

The new HR software is having a few problems. It's slow, and some users can't log in. Nobody knows how to use the software. As part of the project, HR implemented new policies for vacation and paid time off (PTO). These new policies frustrate the users, who blame the problems on the new system. The parking garage has a clear and immediate benefit. It will last for years. No doubt everyone thinks, "What a brilliant investment; we should build more of these." The new HR software generates negativity, and the CEO struggles to understand what she got for her investment.

Is a parking garage more valuable to a company than advanced software to manage people? Of course not. What went wrong? In this example, the HR project was on time and within budget, but it was still considered a failure to some.

The Downward Spiral of Micromanagement

When things go wrong in IT, leaders tighten the screws and micromanage. Table 3.2 provides a list of IT problems and the corresponding unfortunate responses that often follow.

Table 3.2: Common Unfortunate Responses to IT Problems

Problem	Unfortunate response
Project delivered on time and budget but missed the mark on functionality	CIO implements a detailed requirement process that includes user sign-off before work begins.
Project value fails to materialize	CFO implements a strict capital approval process.
CFO questions cost overruns	CIO implements strict time-tracking, so every minute of work is captured and mapped to a project.
Security incident	CIO locks down systems, email, and files. Requires onerous processes for working remotely.
Third-party consultant brought in to analyze IT	CIO overreacts and completely restructures.

Table 3.2: Common Unfortunate Responses to IT Problems *(Continued)*

Problem	Unfortunate response
Pressure from board to stay competitive	CIO agrees to take on multiple large projects at the same time.
Findings on Sarbanes-Oxley (SOX)[4] audit	External consultants are permitted to create oppressive controls.
CEO demands more innovation	CIO ignores technical debt (e.g. legacy systems) and builds new capabilities on a weak foundation.

During the first week of a new job, we had a planned fire drill. While in the stairwell, I overheard two of my new developers discussing the proper way to record the time spent in the fire drill. When I inquired, it turned out that the team was required to account for every minute of their time. When I asked why, several answers were given: (1) it is necessary for Sarbanes-Oxley (SOX); (2) it's required for accounting; and (3) it's necessary for resource planning. None of these answers are accurate, and all of them are frustrating. There are no SOX rules that say you need to document the time salaried employees spend on a fire drill. There are no accounting rules that say you need to document the time salaried employees spend in a fire drill. Micromanaging time is the surest way to destroy productivity. Yes, you must track the time internal employees spend on capital projects. But time tracking should not be extended to lunch breaks, social activities, and fire drills.

As the rules become stricter, the team slows down, and morale dwindles. When a team is not empowered, discretionary effort is gone. The mentality becomes, "If you treat us like babies, we'll act like babies."

When morale drops, people will leave. In any economy, top IT talent is highly sought after, and they can find jobs outside of your company. When morale is low, top talent departs, and the downward spiral continues. As IT delivers less and less, more pressure is put on the CIO, and the screws are tightened another turn.

In an act of desperation, the CIO will cut corners. Usually, the first thing to go is quality assurance testing (QA). Testing is the last thing that stands between development and launching a solution that will be accessed by its users to do their jobs. Cutting corners on QA appears to save time and money, and by squeezing testing, you're merely hoping to still ship a quality solution on time.

This is not a suspenseful story; we all know what comes next. The release is buggy, the users are frustrated by these defects, and the new features create havoc for the customers. Now IT is not just a burden on the bottom line—it is negatively affecting the top line. Fixing these bugs must become the CIO's full-time job, and the dream of being a strategic partner will have to be postponed. Top talent is redeployed to remediation, and the beautiful three-year Gantt chart is quickly turning from yellow to red because you can't move forward when your house is on fire.

At this point, more bad things happen:

- The CIO loses his job.
- The CEO brings in outside consultants to "fix" the IT Department.
- A decision is made to outsource IT.

The chances of an internal candidate becoming the next CIO are slim to none as the internal team is associated with the failures.

The conventional wisdom that you can improve IT by implementing more and more processes and controls is wrong. You may try to combat this by embracing an Agile methodology, but done poorly, Agile can create the same problems. Leaders who micromanage lose their team first and their job second. Trusting and empowering your team is the only way to create an Amazing IT Department.

Four Steps
to Innovate

4

The Right Foundation

When formulating your plan, make sure it's the right plan for your company, your team, and the times. Don't bring what you did at your last job and just impose it on your new team.

Collaborate with your leadership team, and get the right answer together. The same advice goes for this book—it should be used to inform, not direct, your actions. When bringing a new concept forward, take the time to explain the *why*. If it's a technique you had prior success with, tell the story: explain why it worked and what results were obtained. This could take less than 10 minutes and make all the difference in the world.

In building and executing your plan, it is essential that you establish and communicate expectations, trust, and values.

Set Expectations

If you're currently in the market for a new CIO role, you mustn't over-promise during your interview. Even if you were wildly successful in your previous position, it's going to take time to succeed in your new role. Setting expectations too high is a rookie mistake that will be hard to overcome. Straight talk about what it takes to turn around a struggling IT Department will improve your chances of getting and succeeding in the role. If they're expecting the impossible, it's time to move on to the next interview.

If you're a sitting CIO who needs to reset expectations, be embarrassingly overt. Create a new program, give it a name, give it a logo, document it in a strategy, and take it on a roadshow. It is possible to get a second chance in the same job.

To establish a winning leadership approach, you need to become customer-obsessed. Reframe the focus on your stakeholders. How does this help my external customers? How does this help my business partners? How does this help my employees?

When considering your relationships with your boss, your board, and your peers, adjust your communication style to them. Instead of lamenting that they won't take the time to learn your terminology, make it your job to speak in theirs. It's not about meeting them halfway; it's meeting them where they are.

As for your team, you need to trust them. Tech people are smart. Treat them that way. Take the time to share the *why*. Teach them about the business. Make sure they understand the mission, the goals, the long-range plans, and the current results. Go over the numbers with your entire team. Discuss sales results and budget variances. Are these considered a secret in your company? Is SOX used as an excuse to not share this information? If so, then explain that it's a secret. Go over the policy. Explain the risks of insider trading and freeze windows. Explain the corporate policy regarding confidentiality. Remember, you're the leader, and your example will be followed.

Ask your team their opinions about the corporate goals and the plans to achieve them. Let the team shape the solution. Get their buy-in, and they will knock your socks off. We've all been part of a high-performing team in our careers. Teams that have a clear vision, trust, and few roadblocks perform at exceptionally high levels. And let's be honest: Do you think a network engineer who has to record the time they spent in a fire drill is going to spend their personal time thinking of a more reliable way to route traffic in your network?

Build Trust

Trusting your team is critical and a core part of being successful. However, to be trusted, they must be trustworthy. If you have team members with integrity issues, they need to go. If you have team members who are undermining the new plan, they need to go.

If your boss doesn't trust you, you're going to have to move more slowly and bring them along on the journey. You could be new, your boss could be new, or you could have prior missteps that broke trust. Regardless of the reason, lack of trust has to be remedied before you can move forward.

When your team trusts you, they will take the leap of faith with you. Would you rather have someone perform a task because you told them to, or because they're totally bought in and aligned with how they can personally help achieve success? I can assure you, the latter produces much better results.

Share Your Values

Become a philosopher, not a task manager. Talk about your beliefs and values. For example, I believe that people are adults and should be trusted. I believe that the most important role of an IT Department is to "keep the lights on." I believe that the people closest to the work will make the most accurate estimates. Stick to a few core beliefs and values, and repeat them obsessively.

I value teamwork. I value education. I value honest feedback. These are some of my beliefs and values. Yours might be different, and that's fine. Your values will be driven by your knowledge, experience, and goals. Whatever they are, be sure to share them with your organization.

When everyone trusts each other and shares the same values and expectations, you have a firm foundation in place for everything else you do. The Laudato Hierarchy of IT Needs builds further on that foundation, as you'll see in the next chapter.

5 The Laudato Hierarchy of IT Needs

Most people believe that the only thing IT does is implement software to reduce costs or increase sales. When I say "most people," I don't just mean grandmothers and schoolteachers; I mean CEOs, CFOs, and even CIOs.

Listen to the questions you'll get in an interview:

- Tell me about a project that was successful.
- Tell me about a project that failed.
- What's your direct experience with XYZ software?

Here's what they should be asking:

- How do you measure system uptime?
- How should IT measure customer satisfaction?
- What strategies did you use to reduce IT costs?
- What's the process to determine what projects IT works on?
- How important is culture to IT productivity?
- How do you cultivate and nurture innovation?

While *creating value* is the lifeblood of an IT Department, it is only possible when a solid foundation is in place.

Back in school, we all learned about Abraham Maslow's hierarchy of needs.[5] Maslow postulated that in order to achieve love, belonging, esteem, and self-actualization, you first need to satisfy your basic physiological needs — eating, drinking, sleeping — and then your safety needs. If these basic needs aren't met, you will never reach your full potential.

For an IT Department to reach its full potential, I devised a similar model, the Laudato Hierarchy of IT Needs, shown in Figure 5.1.

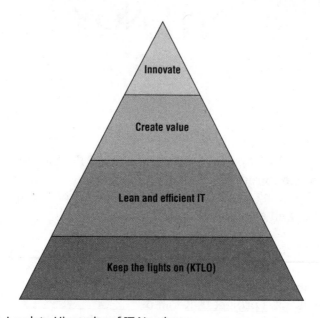

Figure 5.1 Laudato Hierarchy of IT Needs

You can't fall in love while you're being chased by a bear, and you can't deliver value to your company if your systems are crashing, and your costs are out of control. The most important task for any IT Department is building, maintaining, and supporting a secure and reliable foundation.

We'll call this *keeping the lights on*, or KTLO for short. If you think KTLO is someone else's job or something that gets in the way of innovation, you're going to be in trouble. If you think you'll get a seat at the table when the emails aren't emailing and the financial reports are wrong, you're sorely mistaken.

Imagine trying to add a sun deck to your house while your kitchen is on fire. You're happily nailing down the floorboards while your spouse and children are inside screaming. It's not a good look. Obviously, the urgent will outweigh the important, and rightly so. If you're dreaming of having a glass of wine outdoors while the sun sets, you need to get your house in order first. Put out the fire, and then start working on your deck.

6 Keep the Lights On (KTLO)

At Pier 1 Imports, we got so good at the foundation level of the Laudato Hierarchy of IT Needs, KTLO, as shown in Figure 6.1, that I had to fight with my HR business partner to keep it as a metric. Because we consistently maintained 99.9% uptime, he argued that KTLO was solved, and we shouldn't be rewarded for it. I've had a CFO tell me that KTLO is table stakes, and it really "doesn't count" toward CIO effectiveness. CIOs have told me they leave this to their VP of Infrastructure so they can go off and be strategic.

Wrong, wrong, wrong!

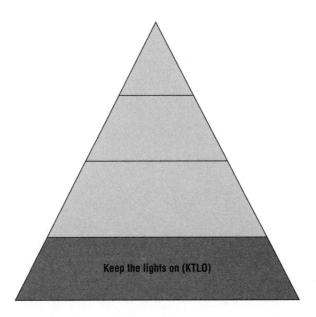

Figure 6.1 Laudato Hierarchy of IT Needs

The moment you get good at KTLO is when you need to double down on it. Complacency is the number-one enemy of reliability. You can only go without air for five minutes, water for three days, and food for maybe a month. If you run out of water, your needs become more desperate, and falling in love goes out the window. If your customer relationship management (CRM) system gets hacked, I promise it's going to occupy your life around the clock until it's resolved. When your engineers are up all night fighting bugs, they're not much use during working hours.

In my blog post "Why CIOs Need to Pour Concrete,"[6] I wrote, "CIOs who understand the need to build upon a concrete foundation will eschew the 'sexy' until their platform is robust, and only then will they create a beautiful and glamorous digital experience built to stand the test of time." KTLO is the key to innovation. It's the foundation upon which it rests.

Once the systems are robust, it's time to move up the Laudato Hierarchy of IT Needs pyramid and create a *lean and efficient* organization.

7 Lean and Efficient IT

A lean and efficient IT Department is a low-cost provider of software and services.

Imagine teaching your kids about money if you have no savings and your credit card debt is mounting. While your advice may be good, your credibility is crap. *Do what I say, not what I do* is a failed strategy for parenting and leadership. Now imagine talking to a senior executive about using technology to drive improvements while your IT budget is out of control. It's the same credibility problem.

As shown in Figure 7.1, we are moving up the Laudato Hierarchy of IT Needs. After getting the foundation solid, the next step is to make IT

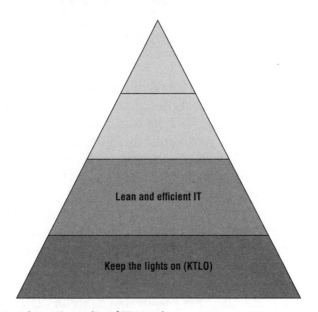

Figure 7.1 Laudato Hierarchy of IT Needs

cost-effective. Get it right, and then get it cheap. Sometimes you have to spend a lot of money to get things stable. Imagine that your website is down because an engineer misconfigured it and then walked out. If the only person who can fix it bills at $500/hour, you grit your teeth and pay the bill. If you need to hire an offshore team to watch your batch systems at night, you grit your teeth and pay the bill. Unreliable systems are expensive.

Place your IT Department on the chart shown in Figure 7.2. If you're in the bottom left, with systems that are both unreliable and expensive, it's time to update your LinkedIn profile. The bottom right—low cost, low reliability—is typical for companies that don't see value in IT. Keeping costs low is the only priority. The CIO probably reports to the CFO in this scenario. Sometimes these companies decide they don't need a CIO, and they turn the function directly over to the CFO.

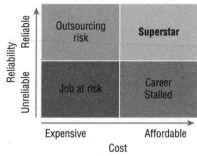

Figure 7.2 CIO Performance Matrix

In the top left, we see the case where things are running smoothly with reliable systems, but costs are above industry averages. This is where outsourcing talk happens. Be wary; the CFO is definitely having a fancy dinner with a global outsourcing company. In other words, if the systems are stable while your costs are above industry averages, you become fodder for outsourcing talk. The CFO and CEO are being approached on a regular basis with the promise of lower IT costs. Once you're externally benchmarked, things get dicey. Benchmarks compare you to everyone, including companies with low IT costs and low IT capabilities. Whether or not it's a well-run IT department becomes irrelevant.

The holy grail is lean and efficient IT. In the top-right box, your team has the time and funding to work on strategic projects. As a superstar leader, you remember that *keeping the lights on* remains the most important priority, so you never lose focus on the foundation as you take the next step up the Laudato Hierarchy of IT Needs pyramid and begin to *create value.*

8 Create Value

"Technology is all I have left."
—Greg Rake, global supply chain expert
Sharing what's going well in his industry, 2020

We are now at *create value*, the penultimate step of the Laudato Hierarchy of IT Needs, as seen in Figure 8.1. When you look at the list of strategic initiatives for your company, how many involve technology? 70 percent, 80 percent, 90 percent or more? Regardless of the industry, technology is at the center of almost all growth plans.

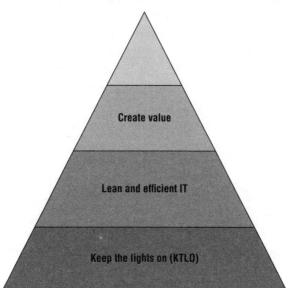

Figure 8.1 Laudato Hierarchy of IT Needs

Digital acceleration is driving these percentages even higher, spurred by the onset of the Covid-19 pandemic in 2020. Digital is transforming all sectors of the economy: manufacturing, media, entertainment, services, education, technology, healthcare, and retail. More and more, your efforts to create value will use and depend on technology in a variety of ways.

That's good to know, but what does it mean to "create value?" In simple terms, creating business value means putting money in the bank. The more successful a company is, the more opportunities exist for its employees. Successful companies invest. Successful companies hire. Successful companies celebrate, and successful companies pay bonuses.

Business value comes from reducing costs, increasing revenue, enabling opportunities, and reducing risk.

Cost Reduction

Cost reduction projects are the easiest to measure, and therefore, the CFO's favorite. One of my favorite cost reduction tools is robotic process automation (RPA). RPA automates repetitive and mundane tasks by replacing work done by people with a software bot. For example, a bot can be programmed to log into a financial system, look up a past-due amount for a customer, format a personalized letter requesting payment, and email that letter directly to the customer. The first time I implemented RPA, I feared a backlash from the people doing the work manually. However, the opposite happened: because the bot replaced the most boring and thankless tasks, people were thrilled and thankful for RPA. Employees could now dedicate their time to more meaningful and fulfilling work.

Increase Revenues and Enable Opportunities

If a company's bottom-line projects are the CFO's favorites, then top-line projects are the CEO's favorite. Projects that increase revenue have much more upside. The sky is the limit on top-line growth. A project that delivers new capabilities can put you ahead of the competition and increase your market share.

In the heat of the Coronavirus pandemic, Vitamin Shoppe commissioned a project to sell on Instacart. Instacart allows a customer to order products on their phone and have them delivered to their home the same day.

It took fewer than 90 days to implement the Instacart project with an exceptional ROI. This is IT at its best. If the tech team had been overwhelmed with KTLO, this project wouldn't have been sanctioned. If IT was over-budget on its capital expenditures, this project wouldn't have been sanctioned. If the prioritization process had been inflexible, this project wouldn't have been sanctioned. And if IT wasn't agile, the project wouldn't have been completed successfully and ahead of schedule.

Some IT projects are known as *opportunity enablers*. Although these types of projects don't have a direct ROI, they are necessary prerequisites to projects that do. A good example would be a content management system for your company's website. The content management system will enable the company to personalize experiences for its customers. Personalization is the real value creator, not the CMS system, itself, that enables personalization. Be sure to combine these types of projects when computing the project's true value.

Reduce Risk

Risk-reduction projects don't directly add to the top line or the bottom line, which sometimes makes them harder for CIOs to justify. Do not let this deter you. Reducing risk is an important undertaking, and projects that reduce risk are arguably more important than projects that fall into other categories. On the infrastructure side of the house, risk-reduction projects include upgrading to supported operating systems, building out redundancy for your network and servers, implementing cyber-security tools, and moving key workloads to the cloud. Applications also benefit from risk reduction efforts. Building fallback systems, modularizing code, and test automation are examples.

Major system failures are costly and embarrassing to companies and harm the reputation of the CIO. Don't wait to reduce risk until after an incident occurs. A mature enterprise risk-management process will help you identify areas of concern for your particular situation.

9

Let's Innovate

To successfully innovate, organizations first need to achieve the bottom three steps of the Laudato Hierarchy of IT Needs: keep the lights on (KTLO), operate a lean and efficient IT Department, and create value for your business.

To foster innovation, you need stable and affordable systems, a process to prioritize projects, and a method to deliver those projects successfully. When IT is a well-oiled machine, it is ripe for innovation, and giant leaps forward will occur. Welcome to the top of the pyramid. As shown in Figure 9.1, it's time to innovate!

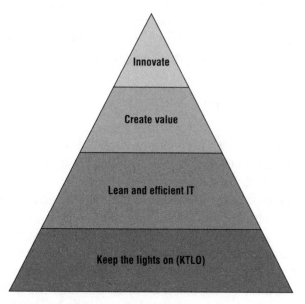

Figure 9.1 Laudato Hierarchy of IT Needs

In 2010, we implemented point-of-sale email receipts at Pier 1 Imports. I was quite excited, and at dinner that night, I bragged about it to my teenage daughter. She looked at me and said, "You didn't already have that?" Clearly, she was not impressed. Omni-channel capabilities like buy online, pickup in store (BOPUS), curbside pickup, ship-from-store, and universal returns don't impress anyone these days. In healthcare, online records, electronic scheduling, and telemedicine are the new norm. Yesterday's innovations are today's expectations.

To invest in innovation successfully, you must be willing to develop an innovator's mindset, dedicate resources, and embrace risk. Only then can you move on to generate ideas, prototype, and turn your vision into reality.

Develop the Mindset

In most companies, especially large ones, a return on investment (ROI) calculation is performed before a project is undertaken. Risks are documented, and contingency plans are drawn up. A project is treated as an investment, and a solid return on the money is expected. Sure, there are consequences for failure: When a project fails, people lose their credibility, their funding, and sometimes even their jobs. However, if you want to be an innovator, you must take calculated risks. When you're able to consider a failed project a valuable learning experience, you have developed an innovator's mindset.

Dedicate Resources

Companies don't innovate; people do. For innovation to work, the company must create a nurturing environment. Sticking a group of people in a room and telling them to innovate is no better than putting a seed on a concrete floor and telling it to grow.

What if you took your best and brightest people away from their day jobs and had them focus 100% on innovation? To even approach this discussion, you must have an extremely reliable infrastructure, a well-managed IT budget, and a steady stream of value creation. In other words, before a CIO can ask the CEO to allocate people and money for a high-risk venture, things better be operating smoothly. On the other hand, if you can only spare the new person and a few interns, your innovation will fizzle. When you're overly reliant on a guy named Brent[7] to keep your systems running, there's no chance he can be assigned to an innovation project.

Embrace Risk

Innovation doesn't exist without risk-taking. If you truly expect to innovate—and to thrive, you better innovate—you must embrace the idea that many of the initiatives you support, fund, and advocate for will be abject failures.

This goes back to the Laudato Hierarchy of IT Needs pyramid: when your foundation is solid, your IT costs are low, and your team is constantly delivering value, you have earned the right to take risks. When taking on a high-risk endeavor, be clear that there is a good chance it may not work. Be confident that the upside is worth the risk, and only *gamble* with the amount of money you can afford to lose.

When you examine today's most successful companies, you can easily correlate their results with their willingness to embrace risk.

Idea Generation

When you're in a good place to innovate, you need to generate ideas. Here are some thought starters on the best places to find ideas:

- Talk to your front-line employees. The employees who deal directly with the customers understand the customer best. Sharon Leite, CEO at Vitamin Shoppe, holds roundtable discussions with store, distribution center, and corporate employees. This keeps Sharon close to the team—and she receives direct insights into what customers are asking for. Innovation is a key pillar at Vitamin Shoppe; it's built into our DNA.
- Survey your customers and ask them about their problems and frustrations. Innovation is problem-solving for consumers.
- Look to other industries: Reed Hastings, the founder of Netflix, was inspired by the gym membership business model before he built the subscription-based DVD business.
- Talk with analysts and thought leaders. They have insight into the trends that are receiving traction with early adopters across various sectors and industries.
- Partner with start-ups. They have good ideas; you have the resources to execute and scale. It's a potential perfect synergy between large and small companies.

- Partner with universities. Students and professors have the knowledge, research skills, and capacity to be terrific innovation partners.

Rapid Prototyping

The mantra of the start-up founder is *fail fast*. This term may sound confusing, because nobody wants to fail, and certainly nobody wants to fail quickly. However, founders understand that to accomplish something truly innovative, they must take risks. They also know that not every idea will be successful, and the quicker they can learn which ideas won't work, the faster they can learn from the failure, iterate, and try the next idea. Failing fast minimizes the time, money, and resources spent on bad ideas.

To accomplish *failing fast* or, hopefully, *succeeding fast*, use a prototype. A prototype is a mockup or partially working sample of the final product. I once worked with a business analyst who mocked up an entire business intelligence dashboard in Microsoft PowerPoint slides. To test the concept, we *pretend clicked* on buttons and then flipped to the page in the slide deck that the actual application would go to when it was completed. This desktop simulation was a quick way to test and iterate the concept before it was built. As an added benefit, the prototype served as a business requirement document for the development team.

The next step in our rapid-prototyping process was to have the development team build a working prototype in HTML. This was still a mockup, but the next step had actual users try the application on a computer. The computer mockup generated more changes, and the process was repeated until an acceptable design was found. If the business intelligence dashboard was a failure, it would be identified during prototyping, preventing us from wasting money on development.

The final step in our rapid prototyping was to build a beta version of the final product: more real than paper and HTML, but still not a full-fledged application. The beta product was released to a limited group of users, monitored, and updated as necessary.

Rapid prototyping ensures the product meets the needs of the customer even if the customer isn't exactly sure what they want in the early stages of the project. In the next chapter, we'll examine how to use these principles to evaluate your IT Department.

10

CIO Report Card

How is your IT Department doing?

I recommend performing an annual IT satisfaction survey of your internal customers (employees and other stakeholders in your organization). When you're a new CIO, perform the first survey immediately, then do a quick follow-up survey after six months. After establishing a baseline, survey once per year as part of your annual review process. Add customer satisfaction as one of every IT leader's objectives—not just the support teams. It's easy to get out of touch in IT; ensuring your team is aligned to their customers will help. Keep the survey short to get a better response. Make it anonymous, and ask open-ended questions to get the best possible feedback.

Grade yourself using the Laudato Hierarchy of IT Needs. To get an A, you need to achieve all four levels. See what the grades indicate in Figure 10.1.

State of IT	Grade	Performance
Stable, affordable, delivering value, and innovating	A	Exemplary
Stable, affordable, and delivering value	B	Above average
Stable and affordable	C	Bare minimum
Cheap and unreliable	D	Not valued
Systems are not stable, and IT costs are out of control	F	Failure

Figure 10.1 The CIO Report Card

III Develop a Winning Culture

11

Culture Eats Eggs and Strategy Eats Bacon, or Something to that Effect

For a long time, I thought culture was some flowery BS spewed by HR types. After all, we were engineers; we did real work. The truth is, I really didn't understand what culture meant.

Culture describes the "norms" of a group. A strong culture can also be an unhealthy culture. See Figure 11.1 to perform a culture evaluation for both your company and your IT department, separately.

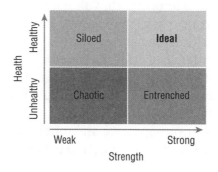

Figure 11.1 Culture Evaluation Matrix

If there is a weak, unhealthy culture (bottom left), you will have high turnover, low productivity, and no discretionary effort. New hires will be discouraged from day one, and top talent will leave even for equal or lower pay. The only way to stay staffed is to overpay to the market. Paying above industry rates for disengaged employees is a recipe for failure. The term *golden handcuffs* is often associated with this scenario. Salaried professionals will behave like hourly workers, starting and stopping according to the clock, not the status of the work. If you have a team of people who always leave the office precisely at 5:00 p.m., you have an unhealthy culture.

Fortunately, I've never been to prison. However, I think of prison when describing a strong, unhealthy culture (bottom right). A high school cafeteria is another one. These are not the places where unique ideas shine through. How you line up, where you sit, and what is discussed are all dictated to you by the culture. These cultures were formed by people who aren't even there anymore. The seniors control the high school culture, and when they graduate, a new group is matriculated to do the exact same thing. This can go on for generations. It's been decades since I've stepped foot into my high school, but I wouldn't be surprised if some of the culture I remember still exists today.

In a weak, healthy culture (top left), while a company has healthy behaviors, they vary from group to group. If your company has more than one location, each one can develop its own culture. An Agile development team may have loose rules about working hours, while other employees follow a strict schedule. Some teams may converse loudly in the aisles, while a group on a different floor is library quiet. I worked in a building where the 7th floor was a party and the 15th floor was a funeral. This could mean you are overdressed on one floor and underdressed on another. Do you have a suit jacket on the back of your door for your trip to mahogany row? That's an example of a company with multiple disparate cultures.

The problem with siloed cultures is that almost all meaningful initiatives require cross-functional collaboration to be successful. For example, to run a successful eCommerce business, you need constant collaboration with Marketing, IT, Supply Chain, Store Operations, and Finance. If all of these groups have different expectations and working styles, it becomes next to impossible and extremely stressful to coordinate across the organization.

A strong, healthy culture is what I witness at Vitamin Shoppe headquarters right now (top right). People are enthusiastic about the work. There is clarity of vision. People go out of their way to help others. Conflicts are debated openly and politely. Our culture is strong, and we see the benefit in positive business results.

This begs the question: Are we winning because we have a great culture, or do we have a great culture because we are winning? It's a bit of both.

You can see this clearly in sports. Winning teams have an us-against-the-world swagger about them. They get the taste of success, and it drives them to work even harder, to support and push each other. They voluntarily get up early to work out and stay late to watch the game film.

Conversely, losing teams play the blame game. In business and sports, leaders often tighten the screws when results are poor. Coach of a losing team: "Go run laps." Manager of a losing team: "Be here at 7:00 a.m. on Saturday."

Here's the bad news: if you try to build an amazing IT culture in a company with an unhealthy culture, it may backfire. In the heyday of the tech boom, companies found it harder and harder to compete for tech talent. Companies like Google and Facebook provided free meals, beer on tap, volleyball pits, and all-you-can-eat M&Ms. I went to a briefing at Microsoft, and there was a cooler full of free Mountain Dew. Free! As a lifelong retailer, lucky to get a free swill of coffee, these perks astonished me.

Many legacy companies decided to mimic these concepts for their IT Departments. Companies installed basketball hoops, ping pong tables, and foosball.

The Wrong Way to Develop Culture

When discussing IT culture, a colleague told me that at TJ Maxx, the IT Department wanted to wear jeans and have more relaxed working hours than the rest of the company. The solution: the company moved IT to a different building.

This story made me cringe: IT volunteered to leave so it could have its own culture. I'm not surprised the company allowed it, since the competition for tech talent is fierce. If jeans and less formal digs help you retain top talent, it seems like an easy trade-off. My guess is that IT was moved to a lower-rent office, saving money in the short term and freeing up space for a revenue-driving function to expand.

While wearing jeans is nice, moving out is a horrible idea. A disconnected IT Department will quickly become more insular, more formal, and less aligned to the corporate goals and culture. Over time, the department will be considered less valuable: a cost and ripe for outsourcing. How does the story end? A quick Google search reveals the unfortunate answer:

TJX Lays Off Hundreds of Employees in IT Restructuring. . . .
as part of this restructuring, certain services will transition to
a third-party provider. – HFN Digital, May 17, 2018

That headline didn't surprise me. For more on my anti-outsourcing opinion, see Chapter 46, "What's Wrong with Outsourcing?"

Building a Strong Culture

When I was interviewing for my CIO role at Pier 1 Imports, I heard a lot about how bad the IT Department was. The consistent theme was that Pier 1 Imports had a unique and special culture, except for IT, which had its own, not-so-wonderful culture. When I asked for an example, the answer was Halloween. Halloween wasn't just another holiday at Pier 1 Imports; it was an event. Costume contests were team efforts, and you didn't just dress up—performance theater was involved. To this day, people still talk about the Finance team's production of *Grease*.

The IT Department didn't participate in Halloween. At all. They had a "culture," but it wasn't in sync with the rest of the company, so there was no connection between IT and everyone else.

I started my job in August, with just two months to fix the Halloween problem. The conversation went something like this:

Me: "Why don't we compete at Halloween?"

IT Director 1: "We're too busy."

IT Director 2: "Our projects are behind; it would look bad."

IT Director 3: "Tech people are introverts. They won't enjoy it."

While all of these sounded reasonable, that didn't matter. Everyone was busy. Our projects were so behind, spending a few days making costumes wouldn't make a difference. And while techies may be introverts, we are also extremely creative and competitive—the perfect skillsets for a costume contest. We went for it. That year, we competed and got an honorable mention. Year two was a tightly contested second place, and in year three, we not only participated, we won Halloween!

My first action as the head of a large IT Department was to convince them to dress up in costumes.

How Can a CIO Influence Culture?

If you find yourself in the same position I did at Pier 1 Imports, with a healthy corporate culture and an unhealthy IT culture, the fix is simple: embrace the corporate culture and align IT to the rest of the business.

If you're at a company with a weak culture or, worse yet, an entrenched, unhealthy culture, your only chance at success is to change the entire company's culture. While this may sound daunting, it must be done.

Fixing IT's culture while leaving the rest of the company behind is a fool's errand. I once believed I could create a beautiful IT culture, and the rest of the company would follow. It doesn't work that way. Purposefully changing IT's culture in a vacuum causes less alignment, more strife, and jealousy from other groups.

Partner with your peers, your CEO, and especially your CPO to create a vision and a roadmap to improve the culture for everyone. This is where you need to remove your CIO hat and put on your corporate executive hat. Can a CIO become the leader who improves corporate culture? Why not? That's what good leaders do.

The Blue Bloods

In college football, there is a select group of teams known as the *blue bloods*: the royalty of college football. Teams like USC, Oklahoma, Ohio State, and Alabama are commonly included in this list. These teams outperform year after year, decade after decade. What makes them consistently great? Is it the coach? No, they all have had success under multiple coaches. Is it the players? No, the players rotate out every four years. What these teams have is a culture of success. A culture of winning. The best coaches are attracted to these programs. The best players are attracted to these coaches. The culture of commitment, dedication, and hard work is passed from upperclassmen to freshmen. The culture supersedes any one person. This should be your goal. Create a winning culture, and you'll build a blue blood IT Department that continues to win long after you've gone out to pasture.

Peter Drucker, a well-known management consultant, educator, and author, is often credited with the popular quote that "culture eats strategy for breakfast." And while sources debate about whether or not it was Drucker who actually used those exact words, the meaning is not often the subject of dispute: a leader could have a solid strategy and a great team, but if the culture won't allow anyone to win, the fruits of success wither and die on the vine.

With a clear vision, a written strategy, and, importantly, a winning culture, the building blocks required for an Amazing IT Department are starting to take shape. In the next chapter, we'll discuss setting up the optimal IT organization structure for your company.

12 The Boxes, the Lines, and the Dashes

For as long as I can remember, I've been obsessed with organizational structures. Creating an optimal org design is critical. Titles and reporting structure matter, even in the most progressive of companies. Who reports to whom, decision rights, and compensation are all determined by the formal organizational structure.

When I became CIO, I spent countless hours working on org design. I went as far as putting names and titles on tiny squares of paper and arranging and rearranging the org chart on the floor of my living room. I believed the perfect structure was out there; I just hadn't found it yet. I was in search of the org equivalent to Einstein's $E=MC^2$, a simple and elegant answer to all of IT's problems. At the risk of pushing my metaphor too far, some of the org designs I've attempted seem more like Schrödinger's equation than the theory of relativity. I finally concluded that there was no such thing as the perfect IT org chart. Every org design comes with trade-offs.

To create the best possible org design for your company's needs, you need to first pretend that everyone on your team died in a fiery plane crash, and start over. Too morbid? Then simply imagine that they all went in on a lottery ticket and hit the jackpot. Whatever mind trick you use, you need to get the existing players out of your head, or you'll end up designing your org around their skills, weaknesses, and aspirations, instead of the needs of your business.

To create your org structure, you first need to understand the work, then build the best structure to organize that work, and finally fill the roles with the best possible people you can get.

Step 1: Identify Your Functions and Business Needs

Document the services you provide to your business. Typical IT Departments perform these functions: strategy, architecture, application development, infrastructure, operations, support, cyber-security, and portfolio/program/project management.

You also need to account for the "business of IT." Budgets, people development, and communications are examples of functions your "IT business" needs. Consider yourself the CEO of IT, and run IT like a business. Now, who's your IT CFO, your IT CPO, and your head of communications? By the way, don't put *CEO of IT* on your business card, since that could be a career-limiting move.

Once you have your direct reports in place, take it down to the next level: e.g., sales apps, financial apps, analytics, supply chain, cloud computing, cyber-security, and operations.

Step 2: Create an Org Chart

Sketch an org chart that best meets those needs. Do not consider people—remember, they are all on a beach drinking Mai Tais. I recommend going down two levels, including directors and managers. If you are designing an Agile organization, this may only include directors, since you typically won't have any managers.

Step 3: Run Use Cases

Run use cases through your draft org design, and determine how well or poorly the following would be accomplished in your new org:

- Creating a three-year strategy
- Adding a new feature to your website
- Prioritizing your project list
- Balancing the IT budget
- A server going down at 3:00 a.m.
- The controller's computer crashing during the month end close

When evaluating the use cases, make sure each is accounted for in your structure. This exercise should pressure-test your org design. If there's a gap, go back to step 2.

Step 4: Identify Skills

Document the skills needed for each position. This is essentially the job description. Write down the mandatory skills and the nice-to-have skills. Are you cheating? Keep those current employees out of your head. (This is why the plane crash works better than the lottery ticket.)

Step 5: Review Your Team

It's finally time to consider the existing team members. Map them to the org chart. Don't force it. If there's a perfect fit between an existing employee and the newly designed role, congratulations: you have the right role and the right person for the job. Where there's a close fit, with one or two missing skills, work with your HR partner to develop a career development plan for that employee. Where you have a role with no qualified internal candidates, it's time for an outside hire. If you have people left over, you have the following options:

- Separate the employee with a severance package. They didn't change; you did.
- Offer a demotion. If there's a better fit in your company, this can be a win-win scenario. Many first-line IT managers will happily go back to being individual contributors if the pay is right.
- Intentionally compromise the structure to match the person. This is not advised, but real life is messier than theory, and I get it. If you do compromise, be honest with yourself and understand the trade-offs.

Next, we'll look a little closer at the org structure and org chart. Chapter 13, "Org Design—Just Show Me the Answer," demonstrates one possible model of an org chart. Chapter 14, "Organization Design and Culture," discusses just how much the org chart does—or does not—matter.

13 Org Design—Just Show Me the Answer

There's no one-size-fits-all IT org chart, but Figure 13.1 shows an example of a design I've had success with.

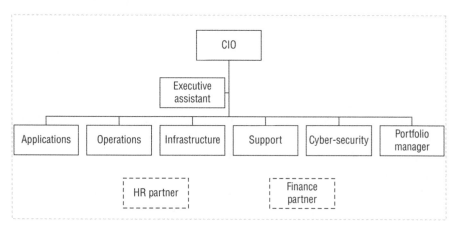

Figure 13.1 Sample IT Organizational Design

Application, Operations, and Infrastructure are all standard CIO direct reports, and I won't delve into those areas. In smaller companies, operations and infrastructure are often combined under one leader. With more and more infrastructure migrating to the cloud, these roles are transforming rapidly.

Support

Back in the early 1990s, one of my mentors, Les Duncan, introduced the idea that the support team (IT help desk and desktop support) should report directly to the CIO. As with many of Les's ideas, at first

I scoffed, only to later see the genius of his ways. Nothing influences the perception of IT inside a company more than your help desk and your desktop support team. This is the only interaction many of your business partners have with IT.

Most of these interactions occur at the most stressful times because computers like to break during the least convenient times. In retail, the help desk is responsible for supporting store systems. Have you ever been shopping, and the register went down? Now imagine being placed on hold with IT and trying to explain the situation while angry customers are lining up. Seconds feel like minutes, and minutes feel like hours. Being told to "reboot and call us back" is not sufficient.

More than anyone in IT, the help desk can empathize with the field employees. They are the window to your internal customers. Staying close to support is key to building an Amazing IT Department. Therefore, the head of IT support should be a member of the IT leadership team and a direct report to the CIO.

Cyber-Security

The case is often made that cyber-security is more comprehensive than just technology, and therefore the CISO should not report to the CIO. In my LinkedIn poll, one-third of the respondents said the CISO reported somewhere outside of IT. In her 2018 article "What's the Best Reporting Structure for the CISO?" Stephanie Overby discusses CISO reporting options in depth.[8] Personally, I believe the CISO should report to the CIO for three reasons:

- The CIO needs to champion, fund, and execute the cyber-security program.
- The CIO is much more skilled at translating cyber-speak to business-speak.
- The CIO needs to own the incident response when something bad happens.

Portfolio Manager

I am not a fan of a centralized project management office (PMO). Instead, I deploy the following model: for teams that have multiple, ongoing projects, I embed a project manager (PM) or scrum master

(SM) on the team. This person is a project management expert in the methodology being used by that team (e.g., Agile, Waterfall, Lean, Kanban) and a subject matter expert in the domain. For teams that don't always have project work, I prefer contract project managers who are also subject matter experts in the specific domain. They come in, do the job, and move on. Whether internal or external, each project needs to fund its own project manager.

I include a portfolio manager on the IT leadership team. The portfolio manager is an individual contributor responsible for the methods, processes, and ceremonies (fancy Agile word for meetings) needed to properly execute the entire portfolio of IT projects. The portfolio manager runs IT prioritization committee meetings and is also responsible for ensuring that projects are being managed consistently across the organization. The portfolio manager coordinates with the embedded project managers in a matrix arrangement providing tools, guidance, and coaching. As tempting as it is, resist the urge to allow your portfolio manager to manage projects. Once you head down that path, it's hard to go back.

HR Partner

I remember the days when HR was divvied up into specialist roles. You went to one person for employee relations (that means something bad happened), another for career development, another for compensation discussions, and so on. This model has evolved, and HR Departments are deploying generalists so that each department head can work with one business partner across all HR disciplines. If you're fortunate enough to work in this model, simply add that person to your extended IT leadership team. Ask them to attend your annual team-building events, offsite planning exercises, weekly staff meeting, and department meetings. When you take your team out to lunch, the HR business partner is invited, too. When you make your HR partner part of the IT leadership team, your team will transform for the better. This is a people job, and HR partners are people experts. In Chapter 32, "Love Your HR Department, Just Don't 'Love' Your HR Department," we'll explore all the benefits of working collaboratively with HR.

Finance Partner

"Money makes the world go 'round," and there is no place this is truer than in business. I've seen IT organizations with an IT controller as a direct report to the CIO. I like that model and see many of the benefits. However, the drawback is that your IT controller may become disconnected from the CFO's org, which is not in your team's best interest. Matrixing a finance person into your team in the same manner as the HR partner is my preferred structure. Yes, they get to go to the team lunch, although they may argue there's no budget for it.

Executive Assistant

We've all moved past *Mad Men*,[9] right? It's not your executive assistant's (EA) job to light your cigarette and get your coffee. Your EA should be a fully contributing member of your IT leadership team.

Here's what to look for in an executive assistant:

- Confidentiality
- Expert-level scheduling skills
- Grammar/writing skills (every writer needs a great editor)
- Basic graphic design skills
- Relationship skills
- Event planning

Your assistant represents you both internally and externally. If it's your goal to be professional, ethical, thoughtful, caring, intelligent, and available, then you need to make sure you have an EA with these qualities. Your assistant should know where you are and where you should be at all times. The more often these two things match, the better your credibility.

14 Organizational Design and Culture

I n a well-run company with an open and trusting culture, the formal org chart doesn't matter as much as it does in other organizations. For example, take a look at the org chart in Figure 14.1. If there's a problem with the wireless network in one of your warehouses, and the manager of warehouse systems works directly with the manager of network operations to resolve it, it doesn't matter who they report to.

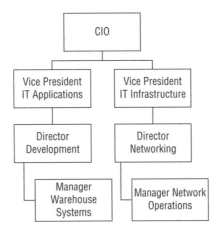

Figure 14.1 Problem Resolution Path Org Chart

If the culture is not so good, this discussion will go up the chain to the directors and possibly the vice presidents. In a worst-case scenario, it will end up on the CIO's desk, and in this example, seven people are now involved. Obviously, the org chart is still helpful. You need to understand each role, its responsibilities, and how it relates to each other so that you can make the right calls. But if your culture is solid, it certainly minimizes the headaches.

15 It's Not the Play, It's the Player

This book contains chapter after chapter on processes and techniques to improve IT success. But given a choice between all of this or a disorganized, chaotic department staffed with spectacular people, I'll take talented people every time. I've seen teams with a disastrous organizational structure drag themselves to success with herculean efforts. I've also seen extremely well-organized teams fail when they didn't have the necessary skill to deliver the results. After all, a project plan can't configure a firewall.

In my experience, the best programmers are 5 to 10 times more productive than an average programmer. Average network engineers may never be able to debug a complex spanning tree issue,[10] no matter how hard they work and how many engineers you have. Would you take four average engineers over two amazing ones? I wouldn't. Want to improve productivity, quality, and morale while *decreasing* the budget? Consider a team with fewer, better people.

Refer to Figure 15.1 to rate individual contributors based on speed and quality.

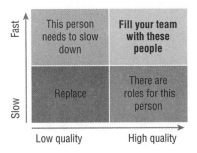

Figure 15.1 Speed and Quality Rating Matrix

Plot each employee on this chart based on the speed and quality of their work. This is not a secret evaluation, unlike the more complex tools commonly used for reviewing talent; show your employee where you have them on this chart. Have the employees place themselves on this chart and compare results.

In the bottom left, we have employees who take a long time to get their work done; and when they finally finish, it's inaccurate. This is an obvious skill mismatch, and these people need to be replaced. In the top right, we have our superstars. They work quickly, and the work is of high quality. Fill your team with these people. If the best of the best are five times better and only cost 25% more, it's smart money to pay at the top of the range for this employee. The low-quality/fast-result crowd (top left) are the toughest employees to coach. They look down on the slow, high-quality employees, but I'll take slow and right over fast and wrong every day of the week. Remember, *if it's not right, it's not done*. Rework destroys timelines. Production bugs erode customer satisfaction. Critical errors put an organization at financial risk. The meticulous crowd that produces high-quality results at a turtle's pace (bottom right) are fine employees if deployed properly. Assign these employees to financial systems, payroll, and similar systems where quality is paramount and speed is secondary.

Once we've identified our top talent, team members who are both fast and good, we need to work hard to keep them motivated, engaged, and on our team. In the next chapter, we'll explore what we can do for them.

16 Take Care of Those Peeps

Take care of your people, and they will take care of you. While it sounds simplistic, employees have two basic rights that should always be honored:

1. The right to know who they report to
2. The right to know what they need to do to be successful

If a software engineer believes that writing a new Application Programming Interface (API) every month is excellent performance, and your basic expectation is a new API every two weeks, you have a mismatch. If that engineer is cube-neighbors with a bossy co-worker, the engineer may be taking direction from the neighbor, not their actual manager. These conditions are morale killers, and they occur more often than you think. While Agile is an amazing tool for developing software, it often creates ambiguity in the reporting structure. Who's in charge: my supervisor, the scrum master, or the product owner? If this is not made clear, the most dominant person becomes the de facto boss regardless of the leader's intent. Above anything else, be sure these basic rights are met for your employees.

Taking care of your people does not mean free Mountain Dew and a foosball table. Those things are nice perks, but they're also superficial. There are 10 tactics for taking good care of your people:

1. Ask people what they want from their career.
2. Spend the most time with your best people.
3. Provide career development planning.
4. Always support your team, even when they're wrong.
5. Be a diode.

6. Have a real open-door policy.
7. Listen.
8. Only make changes that are necessary.
9. Provide fair and timely feedback.
10. Be kind enough to let someone go.

Let's explore these 10 tactics a little further.

Ask People What They Want from Their Career

I realize this is a book on IT leadership, not rocket science; however, here is some advanced advice: just ask people what they want from their career. We're all motivated by different things. Is it money, self-actualization, advancement, responsibility, work/life balance, or making a difference in the world? Ask your team members what they want from their careers, and make a point to help them obtain it.

Spend the Most Time with Your Best People

At one organization where I worked, we had a rock-star IT administrator on our team. He was well-respected and clearly top talent. When I asked his manager how he was doing, the response was, "He's doing great, so I let him do his thing." The IT administrator's manager believed he valued being left alone, and I didn't second-guess this feedback. After all, he was producing outstanding results. Then, one day, the IT administrator resigned. We were all surprised and disappointed. In his exit interview, he confided that he felt ignored and undervalued. He also didn't enjoy various aspects of his job. If we had spent more time with him, we would have known this information.

Managers will benefit more from spending time nurturing top talent than obsessively coaching poor performers. Tobi Barron, an experienced HR business partner, agrees. Tobi explains, "Spend enough time with poor performers to give feedback and coach up—but know when to cut your losses."

Provide Career Development Planning ━━━

Career development planning is a valuable leadership tool. This is not performance management; it's the employee documenting and sharing their personal career goals. Make it your job to help your employees meet and exceed their goals. Understand that sometimes this will be accomplished outside of your company. That's okay; the days of working for the same company from your first job through retirement are long past. Career development planning consists of documenting short- and long-term goals and then creating a plan to attain them following the 70-20-10 model. This model was created in the 1980s at the Center for Creative Leadership in Greensboro, NC.[11] While employees and managers often associate learning and development with formal training, this model demonstrates that only 10 percent of growth comes from formal training; 20 precent is learned from others in various ways; and a whopping 70 percent comes from hands-on experience. If an employee wants to be a project manager, give them the opportunity to manage a project. Institute a career development program for all of your employees, and watch their productivity and morale improve.

Always Support Your Team, Even When They're Wrong ━━━━━━

When I have a new direct report, my first discussion is establishing ground rules for decision-making using the following model:

1. *Do*—Decisions you make without my knowledge
2. *Inform*—Decisions you make and let me know about
3. *Ask*—Decisions you discuss with me in advance

As an executive, I don't want to know about every little thing. If you bring minutia to me, I'm going to question why I need you on my team. As a vice president, director, or manager, you have decision rights, and you are paid to use them.

On the other end of the spectrum, if you start making big decisions without my consent or knowledge, we could get sideways quickly. When you make mistakes, it's my job to support you, and I can only do that when I'm in the loop. The mantra I learned from Cary Turner, with whom I worked for many years, was "NO SURPRISES!"

I direct my new subordinates to err on the side of informing. Move forward and let me know. This allows us to move quickly and prevents me from both being a bottleneck and being blindsided. I promise that when I'm properly informed, I will have your back. If I disagree or think something was a mistake, we will discuss it in private. This technique quickly builds trust, and over time the right balance of *do/inform/ask* becomes optimized.

This model works both ways. Each time you report to a new boss, have this conversation. All leaders have a different level of comfort on this scale. I've reported to a leader who was squarely in the "ask first" bucket. This evolved to "inform" as we developed trust.

Be a Diode

We've all heard of diodes, at least the light-emitting kind (LED). What does this have to do with taking care of your employees? A diode is an electronic device that allows electricity to travel freely in one direction while blocking travel in the other direction. Our beloved computers rely on diodes to operate. The leadership analog is to allow praise to flow right through you to your team. When things go well, don't bask in the glory: instead, celebrate the people who did the work. For criticism and blame, do just the opposite: ensure that those stop at you. You're in charge, and you're responsible. When leaders pass the praise and accept the blame, they are taking care of their team, and it won't go unnoticed.

Have a Real Open-Door Policy

I've never met a leader with an official closed-door policy. Every leader claims to be available to their team. How is this accomplished when you're in back-to-back meetings from early morning through the evening? Here are some tactics for implementing a real open-door policy.

Start with your executive assistant (EA). Be certain your assistant knows that anyone who wants to meet with you from your extended team is a priority. EAs are magicians, but they need to know your priorities. Don't let a fast-talking salesperson take time away from your team. Make yourself available to your team outside of normal work hours; early or late meetings work well for this. Do you still go to work in the office? A phone call during your commute is another opportunity to have a fruitful discussion. Be approachable. Get out of your office. If the behavior changes when you enter an area, that's a sure sign you aren't coming around enough. When people joke, "Watch out, the boss is coming," you have a problem. If you have a corporate cafeteria, make it a point to eat lunch there frequently. The kitchen is a favorite casual meeting place. Get your own coffee. Hold roundtable breakfasts with random people from your department. Schedule your one-on-one meetings in your subordinates' office. When you get out of your office, team members will see you more often, which improves your approachability.

Be mindful of these efforts. After reading an article about the benefits of *management by walking around* (MBWA),[12] I began making rounds of the IT Department at the end of my day. The problem? Since I was wandering the halls between 5:30 and 6:30 p.m., it appeared as though I was checking on who was still working. Soon people stayed late so I would see them at their desk when I made my rounds. My good intentions backfired. MBWA works much better at 10:00 a.m. than at 6:00 p.m.

In a work-from-home (WFH) model, we have to be more intentional. One of the biggest downsides of our virtual world is the lack of chance encounters. Scott Devlin, vice president of applications at Vitamin Shoppe, championed skip and super-skip meetings. On a quarterly cadence, Scott holds one-on-one meetings with all 45 members of his extended team.

Listen

I know I'm biased, but IT Departments are full of smart people. On top of that, IT people are creative. When you combine creativity and intelligence, good idea after good idea emerges. Our job is to create an environment where these ideas can be heard.

After getting feedback on a 360 review, I worked with an executive coach to improve my listening skills. My coach had me keep score in meetings. I counted every time I asked a question and every time I made a statement. After a week, we reviewed the results. I had made three statements for each question I asked. The coach challenged me to flip the ratio—to ask three or more questions for every statement I made. With the help of my coach, I learned to ask questions and listen to the answers.

Agile and Lean[13] practitioners have embraced a concept called *The Five Whys.*[14] *The Five Whys* is a method of asking questions until you get to the root cause of the problem. Parents are experts at using five whys:

1. Why didn't you do your homework? *My laptop is broken.*
2. What's wrong with your laptop? *It won't charge.*
3. Why won't it charge? *My charger quit working.*
4. What happened to your charger? *It got wet.*
5. How did it get wet? *I left it outside in the rain* (root cause).

When a leader makes a statement, it ends the discourse. A question continues the discussion and deepens understanding. Another helpful technique is to have the lowest-ranking person in the room speak first. For example, have the junior network engineer give their opinion before the VP of infrastructure, the CIO, and the COO.

Paul Demboski, a successful business leader, likes to respond to statements with the phrase "tell me more." *Tell me more* is a simple yet powerful comment that encourages more robust discussions.

When you listen to your team, you'll get better ideas and better results, and you'll earn their respect in the process.

Only Make Changes that Are Necessary

You say "toe-may-toe," I say "toe-mah-toe." When reviewing your team's work, don't recommend changes simply because it's not how you would have done it. By all means, correct errors and suggest meaningful improvements, but don't nitpick at the work. When you're constantly making small, irrelevant changes, you undermine your subordinates and waste your own time.

Provide Fair and Timely Feedback

The best feedback is given as soon as practical after the occurrence. If your dog goes to the bathroom in your living room, you don't wait until the annual review to give him an unsatisfactory score on house training. It's a similar concept at the office. The best feedback is specific, timely, and personal. For example, "This morning, when you told the customer to buzz off, I was shocked and embarrassed." Give this feedback in private, as soon as possible. By making the feedback about your personal feelings, you take away any arguments. It's hard to argue about another person's feelings. Your subordinate is not in a place to say that you didn't feel embarrassed. Follow up with constructive advice on possible alternatives to the action in question. Once the feedback is given and received, move on. We're all human, and we're all learning.

As a leader, it's your responsibility to provide feedback. Fair and honest feedback is a gift that all employees deserve.

Be Kind Enough to Let Someone Go

The worst job responsibility for any manager at any level is letting someone go. When an employee is in the wrong role, and coaching and training are not sufficient, the best thing you can do for that person is to separate them from the company.

Don't believe me? I encourage you to speak with people who have been in that situation. In fact, most end up better off. When the authors of *The CEO Next Door* tracked more than 2,600 executives over a 10-year period, they discovered something startling: of those who were fired, an incredible 91 percent ended up finding a new position that was as good as or better than their last.[15]

I know several people who look back on losing their job as the "kick in the pants" that motivated them to pursue a career doing something they loved. Moving a poor performer from team to team is not good for your company, not good for your managers, and certainly not good for the struggling employee. Sometimes, taking care of your people means having the courage to let them go.

17 Hire the Best

Before you decide to replace poor performers, be sure you understand why their performance is suffering. Do you have a manager who is creating the poor performance? If so, you need to change the manager, not the individual contributor. Do you have a culture that's creating poor performance? If so, your next hire will fail as well, and your reputation as a bad place to work will be enforced.

Are you able to identify top talent during your interview process? In the book *Topgrading*, by Brad Smart,[16] Smart makes the point that replacing existing "C" players with new "C" players is worse than taking no action at all.

When hiring, I look for four key attributes:

1. Integrity
2. Intelligence
3. Ambition
4. Temperament

Notice that I didn't say five years of Oracle database administration or a Scaled Agile Framework (SAFe) certification. While job-specific skills can be taught, I can't teach people to be honest, smart, and driven. I can't make you good-natured—if you completely lose it every time something goes awry, there's nothing I can do to modify that behavior. These characteristics are innate, or perhaps you learned them before you were five years old. Either way, by the time I meet you, it's too late.

Integrity is non-negotiable. Without integrity, everything else falls apart. Warren Buffet once said, "If you hire someone without [integrity], you really want them to be dumb and lazy."[17]

When you're building a team of superstars working together to achieve the common goal, it's important that the team members are driven to succeed. The aptly named Coach Winn, a two-time Olympian, national coach of the year, and best-selling author, calls these driven people *separators*. "Most people just do the givens and expect what the separators have. Separators do the things that nobody else is willing to do. This is the key to their success."

When I interview, my job is not to find reasons to hire the candidate—it's my job to find a reason *not* to hire the candidate. As the leader, I consider my role in the interview process the veto role. HR and first-round interviewers should evaluate the candidate for the technical prowess, and unqualified candidates should never get to the CIO.

One of my favorite interview questions is a simple math question:

What is three plus four times five?

I don't really care if the candidate knows the answer or not; I care about how they consider the question. If you're being asked this question, you should probably pause and consider that there's a reason it's being asked. Pausing is a sign of emotional intelligence. If you blurt out "35," I'll politely explain that that is not the correct answer. Sometimes candidates get angry or call my question unfair. They'll ask about parentheses, or they'll keep guessing. The next most common answer I get is 60. I've asked this question a lot, with the top wrong answer being 35 and the second most common wrong answer being 60. Why 60? Because after $(3+4) = 7$, then $7 \times 5 = 35$ is wrong, the candidate remembers the order of operations but forgets the plus sign. So, now flustered, they wrongly compute $(4 \times 5) = 20$, $20 \times 3 = 60$.

If you tell me 35 or 60, no worries; you still have a chance at the job once we talk the problem through. However, if you get angry, call my question unfair, disagree with the final result, shun the order of operations, or demand that I provide parenthesis, I'm not going to hire you. The answer to this problem is 23. The order of operations dictates that multiplication comes before addition: $4 \times 5 = 20$, and then $20 + 3 = 23$. Candidates who give me an answer other than 23, 35, or 60 definitely concern me because they're failing at basic math. (On occasion, I interview a math person who calmly says "23" and doesn't understand why the question is difficult. In this case, I need to find another question to apply pressure to the candidate. I have my favorites, but I'm keeping them to myself. If you'd really like to know, send me a message.)

We want team members who have grace under pressure. Any question that puts pressure on the candidate will help reveal a tiny bit of their character.

As you grow and expand your high-performing team, be sure to make diversity a cornerstone of your approach. In the next chapter, we'll discuss the benefits of a diverse team.

18

The Best Team Is a Diverse Team

The results are in, and the best-performing teams are diverse teams. This is especially true when it comes to innovation. "In a study conducted using a sample of 7,600 London-based firms, researchers found that "companies with diverse management were more likely to introduce new product innovations than are those with homogeneous *top teams.*"[18]

I'm very inclusive when it comes to diversity. Age, gender, race, background, education, and sexual orientation are all included. Different perspectives add to the conversation, creating more robust discussions. Even if you're not concerned about the economic benefits of diversity, consider these other benefits:

- It's the right thing to do.
- It's more fun to be on a diverse team.
- The food at the potluck is better.

All kidding aside, most of us can and should do better in this area. Lack of diversity is a significant challenge in the technology sector. Techpact.org was founded by a group of forward-thinking IT leaders to "reduce the digital divide and pursue representative diversity in technology across all levels." As you look to improve diversity in your organization, TechPact.org is a valuable resource.

To build a diverse team, you need to rethink old paradigms: see Table 18.1.

Table 18.1 Updating Your Thinking Paradigms

Old thinking	New thinking
I'm more comfortable around people similar to me.	People from different backgrounds and experiences will enhance our team's creativity.
Improving diversity is HR's job.	Building the best possible team is the job of the leader.
There aren't enough diverse candidates.	I need to seek out diverse candidates.
This job requires a college degree.	Let's hire based on character and aptitude.
What I've done in the past was successful.	The world has changed; I need to change with it.

Hiring the best and embracing diversity is necessary but not sufficient. In the next chapter, we'll explore the best way to use external resources to further augment your team.

19 Using Mercenaries— I Mean, Consultants

Consultants are people too, and there is value in using external resources strategically in an organization. When used wisely, external resources provide knowledge, skills, and perspectives that your internal team doesn't have. Want to implement a new payroll system? Hire a partner who's already successfully implemented the same system multiple times. Adding experts to a project is a smart business practice. When considering external resources, you should always weigh the cost-benefit like any other investment. All consultants are expensive, and some are ridiculously expensive. However, like a fine wine, sometimes they're worth it.

Management Consultants

Management consultants are high-dollar firms that provide broad business strategies. These firms are commonly hired at the CEO or board level when a complete change in direction is desired or required. These engagements cost millions or tens of millions of dollars. If the counsel provided is the difference between a successful transformation or Chapter 11 bankruptcy, then the money will be well spent. Management consulting firms hire the best and brightest, and they have mad PowerPoint skills. These companies are thriving. Bain and McKinsey have annual revenues of over $4 billion and $10 billion, respectively.

We've all heard the quip that management consultants will ask to borrow your watch, tell you what time it is, and then sell the watch back to you. Extracting and exploring existing ideas is the best thing management consultants do. They interview key personnel at your company, dig into the numbers, and review processes. During these interviews, your company's experts finally have a platform to recommend their ideas and solutions. Ideas that have gone unheralded for years finally see the light of day. Management consultants package the good ideas, along with industry best practices, into a well-organized presentation. They estimate the costs, resources required, and timing to carry out the initiatives needed to turn your business around. And—surprise, surprise—they have the team required to implement these initiatives.

Project-Based Consultants

Project-based consultants operate on the execution side of consulting—implementing the strategy once executive leadership approves it. These firms offer comprehensive solutions, including program management, business analysis, technical resources, and change management experts. They are known in the industry as system integrators (SIs) and have expertise in one or more software solutions. It's not uncommon for prominent software vendors to bring a preferred SI to the table during the initial sales process.

The project-based model works best when the CIO takes an active role in the management of the partner. If you think you can sign the agreement and switch your focus to another priority, this project will be a mess quicker than you can say, "It's time to update my resume."

The most common commercial models for SIs are time and materials (T&M) and fixed-bid. In a T&M arrangement, the CIO needs to control project costs at the line level. Don't agree to a blended rate. Don't allow your consultant to live high on the hog on your travel budget. Either require them to follow your internal travel guidelines or, my preference, ask for an all-in rate so you don't get frustrated when you see them eating Beluga caviar at The Ritz-Carlton.

In the T&M model, you pay an hourly rate for each hour spent, plus the travel as mentioned. If you didn't expressly prohibit it in the contract, don't be surprised when you see charges for back-office admin work, copies, and office supplies. This is the materials part of time and materials.

Know what you're paying for before the project begins. I've seen the SI's top dogs bill outlandish rates when they grace you with their presence. In the 1990s, I led a project that held a monthly quality review with the SI. The lead partner attended these meetings and billed us

$400 per hour for her time. In one two-hour meeting, I counted seven words spoken by the partner. That's $114 per word. She was impressive, but not that impressive. I've seen hours billed by salespeople when they show up to pitch more work. I've seen hours billed for travel time from Europe to the US. I'm not bashing the SIs for these practices; I'm panning the CIOs, like myself, who allow it. Spend your project budget on the project managers, business analysts, product owners, UX designers, software engineers, and quality assurance specialists doing the real work.

When negotiating a T&M contract, insist on complete authority over staffing. It's your project, and if someone doesn't fit in, you shouldn't hesitate to have them removed. These are not employees, and they are not entitled to the same level of due process. People aren't fungible: don't allow the SI to swap out people indiscriminately.

The classic project management tool, *earned value*, is useful in a T&M project. Make sure the work is completed and the dollars spent are in line. If you've spent 80 percent of your budget and completed 60 percent of the work, the time for a red flag is now. While the project isn't officially over budget yet, it certainly will be soon.

In a T&M contract, the longer the project goes on, the more money the SI makes. The more problems you have, the more money the SI makes. The more rework, the more money the SI makes. The more the scope expands, the more money the SI makes. This business model can be conflicting to the goal of delivering the project on time and on budget. Here's an old lawyer joke I've adapted to IT:

What's the difference between a good consultant and a bad consultant?

A bad consultant may let a project drag on for years. A good consultant knows how to make it last even longer.

A fixed-bid contract is sometimes offered to counteract these challenges. In this arrangement, an up-front agreement is made about scope. When the work is complete, there is a user acceptance sign-off, and the SI is paid in full at the agreed-upon price. Anyone who's bought a new home from a commercial builder is familiar with this model. You lock in the scope before construction begins, and changes are handled through a change-order (more money, more delays) process. In fixed-bid, if the price of shingles increases during construction, that's on the builder. The builder takes on risk with the promise of a financial upside when everything goes well. The problem with fixed-bid for IT projects is that we seldom know what the final product should look like before a project begins. Fixed-bid is designed to punish changes. Fixed-bid projects require extensive documentation and clarity about what's in scope. These partnerships become contentious when there is disagreement about what was delivered versus what was specified. "Working as designed" does not mean it's meeting the business needs. CIOs involved in fixed-bid contracts need to become intimately familiar with the terms of the contract.

My favorite commercial model for a system's implementation is a hybrid of T&M and fixed-bid. I learned this from Les Duncan when we were implementing SAP at Jo-Ann Stores in 1998. The arrangement was that the agreed-upon hourly rate would decrease by a percentage every week that the project was delayed beyond the original date. Once the due date passed, the declining margins disincentivized the SI to drag the project out. A financial reward for early completion was also included. A similar model is commonly used for road construction projects.

When you hire the right project-based consultants and actively manage the relationship, a win-win model can emerge. Amazing CIOs forge partnerships where the project's success benefits all parties. These partnerships can continue for years, with internal and external team members working together to continuously deliver value for their respective organizations.

Offshore, Nearshore, Onshore

The cost of living varies widely around the world, which has created a global market for talent. Offshore, nearshore, and onshore are all business models that offer less expensive resources than you can find in your backyard. This is made possible through the relative ease of working remotely. The 2020 coronavirus pandemic accelerated remote-working capabilities, making the market for tech talent truly global.

India has long been the star of this type of outsourcing. India offers strong technical proficiency, English language, and lower wages. India's culture and employment model make it more difficult for Indians to switch jobs. Lower turnover improves team continuity and keeps wages down. The Ukrainian government promotes both technical education and English, making Ukraine another strong option for outsourcing.

In the nearshoring model, outsourcing companies promote time zone proximity as an advantage. In the US, examples are Canada, Mexico, and Brazil. Also, in the US, onshore centers are popping up in more affordable cities than the traditional tech hubs like San Francisco, Seattle, Boston, and New York City.

The downside to all of these models is the dissonance created by different cultures and motivations across the teams. Many concepts are lost in translation. Colloquialisms, sarcasm, and cultural references need to be removed from conversations. Both Waterfall and Agile methodologies promote close proximity as a core advantage for teams. When the team is on the other side of the world and sleeping while you're working, this challenge has to be overcome. Before choosing an outsourcing model, CIOs need to weigh the benefits and ensure the savings are important enough to make up for the loss in team cohesion. I'm a fan of staffing your teams with fewer, better people. Even in an outsourcing model, this is a critical concept. Armies of average developers, no matter how cheaply they come, are not the answer to creating a world-class IT Department. If your only factor in picking a partner is the hourly rate, you are in for a disappointment. I've had a management consultant suggest IT savings by recommending that I replace my long-time incumbent offshore partner with a lower-cost team. This advice is beyond horrible. Whether your team is in India, Ukraine, or College Station, Texas, these are people we're talking about; and as I previously mentioned, people are not fungible. Team cohesion, trust, and norms all take years to establish, and blowing all of that up for $2 an hour is not advisable, to put it nicely.

When done well, targeted outsourcing creates a competitive advantage. Finding, nurturing, and keeping a dedicated, talented, integrated team of outsourced resources can add tremendous value to your team.

Staff Augmentation

The simplest and most straightforward outsourcing arrangement is staff augmentation. In this model, individual contractors are hired for a specified period. The contract employee works side-by-side with the team in roles similar to employees. An hourly rate is paid directly to the contractor or a staffing company that sources and provides talent. This arrangement works well when you need a specific skill for a short time. Generally, in these arrangements, the company has a right to hire these contractors for a fee that declines to zero over time. This allows a try-before-you-buy model that lets both the company and the employee ensure there's a fit before making the relationship more permanent. There are a few things to watch out for in this model. If you don't manage staff augmentation properly, local, state, and federal governments may consider these contractors your employees. A team of contractors will not become as ingrained in your culture as employees; and since you're paying a markup, this model is more expensive than hiring your own staff.

I am a strong proponent of contract employees. When used wisely, they can quickly bring needed expertise to your team. If you're looking to get into this type of arrangement with a staffing firm, it's not difficult. Just wait a few minutes, and you'll get a call, email, or LinkedIn InMail from your friendly neighborhood account representative.

Boutique Firms

There's an old IT adage: *you won't get fired for hiring IBM*. It's based on the theory that a CIO can cover their behind by hiring a big-name firm. This is a losing mentality. Hire the best partner for the job. There is no need to place blame when a project succeeds.

If you value the capabilities of a consulting firm more than its pedigree, you may find benefit using a boutique firm. Boutique consulting firms specialize in just one or two specific disciplines where they are very experienced. With a boutique firm, you work directly with the principals, and your project means more to them than it does to the big guys. Boutique firms are harder to find since they don't have a large sales staff or marketing budget. A referral from another CIO is the best way to identify a talented boutique for your next project.

Whether you're hiring a by-the-hour contractor or entering into a multi-million-dollar engagement with a management consulting firm, take an active role in negotiating terms that lead to a successful outcome for all parties. Use your network to find partners. When looking for a perfect match, there's nothing more valuable than a referral from another CIO.

In the next chapter, we'll discuss how strategic partnerships accelerate innovation.

20 The Power of Experts

O ne of my career highlights was a predictive analytics project I worked on in partnership with the big data analytics firm MAX451.[19]

Not that long ago, a company would put out the same offer to all of its customers. For example, PetSmart would email their entire database an offer for *25% off dog food*. The problem is that some of their customers had cats, fish, or frogs. Cat people considered the offer irrelevant and opted out from further messages. They might even get irritated with the company: "You know I have a cat; why do you keep sending me dog offers?"

Over time, companies got smarter and began segmenting customers. I'm guessing "pet_type" is a field in PetSmart's customer database, and now only dog people get dog offers. This is a good start, but it falls apart for big-ticket items. Once you decide to make a large purchase, like a new laptop, your social media and inbox will magically begin filling up with laptop offers. Are they listening in on your conversations, or reading your mind? That's a topic for another time, but you're searching, and they know it.

You do your research, make your decision, and buy that laptop. What happens next? You continue to get laptop offers for months after the purchase. Unlike dog food, you only buy a computer once every few years, so the ads are ineffective. The company needs to know what you will buy *next*.

At Pier 1 Imports, when a customer bought a dining table, we didn't want to continue pushing dining tables at that customer. So, what's next? Perhaps it's dinnerware to serve on top of the new table. Maybe not; maybe the table was part of a dining room project, and now the customer is searching for a hutch or a side table. Who knows? I'm just guessing, and so were we.

This was the challenge I took to MAX451 CEO Kristian Kimbro Rickard. Rickard explained that this was the perfect business problem for machine learning. With the right model and enough data, the algorithm can predict the next purchase with better accuracy than legacy algorithms. At the time, I believed the only way to process this much data was to build your own Hadoop environment. This meant onsite servers, storage, and cobbling together open source software. A big data project of this magnitude was beyond the appetite and budget of a home furnishing retailer.

As a boutique firm, on the leading—some say bleeding—edge of big data and machine learning, Rickard knew that Microsoft was building big data and machine learning capabilities into its Azure cloud. As an expert, she had the connections and clout to get our project into a private beta program with Microsoft. This is not something I could have done on my own. My local Microsoft team wasn't even aware of the corporate beta program.

MAX451 brokered the arrangement. Microsoft would provide the environment and data scientists; Pier 1 Imports would provide the data and the business expertise; and MAX451 would manage the project, translate between the business and technical experts, and keep everyone on track. Microsoft was on a strict timeline, requiring a successful case study before its Azure big data product launched. We moved quickly, with tangible results in only six weeks. In a short period, and with a small investment, Pier 1 acquired the ability to send more relevant offers to its customers.

In projects like these, everyone is a winner. Pier 1 came away with a groundbreaking solution, MAX451 expanded its reach and credibility, and Microsoft got its case study[20]. This story went viral: Microsoft published case study videos featuring Pier 1 executives and our partner, MAX451, walking through the personalized marketing use case scenario and resulting analytics solution,[21,22] and articles in *Information Week*,[23] *CIO.com*,[24,25] *Chain Store Age*,[26] *Retail TouchPoints*,[27] as well as other retail and technology publications quickly followed.[28] Although this was back in 2014, elements of this end-to-end data and analytics solution is still considered groundbreaking today.

Whether you're working with a multibillion-dollar consulting firm or the smallest boutique, the key is finding the right people. Kristian Kimbro Rickard took the time to understand our business needs before she recommended a solution.

Too often, people show up with technical answers, searching for a business problem. I'm often asked, "What's your cloud strategy?" At Vitamin Shoppe, we have a business strategy that we will execute using the cloud. That's not a cloud strategy; it's a health and wellness strategy. The difference here is not subtle. As CIOs, we need to solve business problems. Finding partners who ask the right questions before they offer a solution will put you on the right path to accomplishing that goal.

People are key to your success. In the next chapter, we'll explore how to build a robust people network.

Build that Network

It's not uncommon for people to send me a LinkedIn request the day after they lose their job. While networking is the key to landing your new role, the time to start building a network is long before you need it. As networking advocates like to say, "You need to dig the well before you're thirsty."

The most important network for a CIO is other CIOs in the same industry. In the 2000s, there was a thriving retail community in the Dallas/Fort Worth metro area, and the retail CIOs got together frequently. These get-togethers were almost always dinners organized by professional connectors and paid for by IT vendors. Professional connector Cathy Hotka built an entire business around connecting retail leaders. Not only does Cathy arrange the dinner, pick the menu, and invite the right mix of people, but she shows up in person and keeps the conversation flowing. Cathy ensures that everyone has a say and nobody dominates the discussion. She gently coaches her paying customers about networking etiquette, strictly prohibiting PowerPoint presentations and other overt sales tactics. If you work in retail, you need to be on Cathy's list. If you work in another industry, you need to find your version of Cathy Hotka. If there isn't a Cathy, start your own CIO networking group.

When I worked for Pier 1 Imports, Andrew Jackson, the president and co-founder of BravoTECH, came to me with a proposition. Andrew would hold a monthly IT leader roundtable in my office. He would set the topics, invite the guests, and buy the breakfast. All I had to do was provide the venue and attend the meetings. These monthly meetings were fun and informative. They took place from 7:30 a.m. to 9:00 a.m. in my office building, so the time commitment was nominal. Depending on the topic, I would invite different members of my IT leadership team to attend. Never once did Andrew or his team try to sell at these meetings. Andrew knew that long-term relationships were a key component of business success.

To start your own networking group, I recommend that you approach a third-party connector like Cathy Hotka, or an IT vendor like Andrew Jackson, to manage and fund the events. I once believed we CIOs could arrange our own networking breakfasts and dinners, but there's more to it than meets the eye. Hosting a CIO IT networking event is complex and time-consuming. If you're looking to host or join a CIO roundtable, I strongly recommend partnering with an expert.

The coronavirus pandemic has moved networking to video conferencing. This new model makes attendance easier, less regional, and more affordable. However, side conversations and interpersonal connections are lost on video, and I believe that post-pandemic, in-person networking events will return and remain as important as ever.

Formal CIO Networks

If your company participates in an industry association, there's a good chance that group has a CIO Council. Specific industry councils are not only valuable due to the commonality of challenges and needs—a well-organized CIO committee can come together to impact meaningful change. The National Retail Federation (NRF) CIO Council has championed standards for years. Standards allow a barcode scanner from company A to work seamlessly with a cash register from company B. These standards help everyone, including the consumer, and they help to move our industry forward. In healthcare, the College of Healthcare Information Management Executives (CHIME) has successfully influenced regulations, improving the implementation and use of electronic healthcare records.

When participating in these organizations, CIOs need to put the interest of their own companies first. Don't allow your advocacy work to trump your day job. Get approval from your CEO before you get involved; and represent the position of your company, not your own position. Where they differ, I recommend recusing yourself from the debate. It's most likely your title got you in the room, not your bubbly personality.

I'm the first to admit that these events can be intimidating. When I first walked into an NRF CIO Council meeting 20 years ago, I was more nervous than a turkey the week before Thanksgiving.

These CIOs were impressive people from impressive companies, and they all seemed to know each other. CIOs are sharp, cynical, and a bit jaded. The meeting was run with a touch of formality, kicking off with anti-trust guidelines and a word from the NRF's general counsel. You put all this together, and it's a bit daunting. However, once the conversations started, I realized I was at home with this group as we all shared a great deal in common. This annual meeting became the most important meeting I attended all year, and the friendships I have developed through these meetings will last a lifetime.

The best way to participate in roundtable discussions is to share accomplishments. I don't care about what you're planning to do in the future. After all, any idiot can sign a contract. If you've successfully implemented a new order management system or rolled out SD-WAN to hundreds of remote locations, I want to hear all about those accomplishments. Some people attend roundtables and don't say a word. Others don't stop talking. Find a happy balance, and you and your peers will get the most from your attendance.

Navigating a Cocktail Party

Like many IT professionals, I consider myself a reluctant extrovert. At an industry party, I'd much rather sit in the corner and chat with a few friends than mingle among the crowd. When you pay to attend, take time away from the office, travel across the country, and then only talk to the staff person you brought along so you wouldn't be alone, it's bad for your business, and it won't grow your network.

If you're an introvert, consider attending these conferences alone. Bringing a co-worker along makes it easy to avoid networking. You can talk to your co-workers for free back at the office.

Here are a few tips to successfully navigate a cocktail party:

- Try sparkling water and lime—at most, have one drink to calm your nerves, but this is not the time or place to get inebriated. (I know: do what I say, not what I do. I'm older and wiser now.)
- When salespeople approach you, ask them to introduce you to another CIO or industry peer. Let the extroverts do their thing to your advantage.
- Have a goal of making at least one new peer contact per day of the conference. Get contact information, and send a follow-up email

the next day. Don't wait until you get home. You'll quickly be distracted by the backlog of work that piled up while you were away.

Now that we've proven the efficacy of remote working, CFOs are going to question the value of conferences. I recommend keeping and publishing detailed notes about what you learned and the people you met at the show. Send this to your direct reports and your executive leadership team upon your return. Just one new idea, or one pitfall avoided, will easily pay for your trip. Formatting and editing your notes is a good activity on the flight home. It's not too nerdy to calculate an ROI for your attendance. If this was your money, would you have still gone?

Finally, if you really just need a break from the grind, take your family on vacation instead. You can afford it, and I'm betting you have a pile of unused PTO.

Social Media

If you think networking means sending friend requests to random CEOs on Facebook, you need to re-read this chapter. Social media is a valuable tool, but it doesn't come close to actual conversations between people. In Table 21.1, I share my approach to social media (knowing full well that there are various and different ways to maximize value from these tools).

Table 21.1: Networking and Social Media

Social media	Usage
Facebook	Friends and family only. I use it to keep in close contact with people I know in real life. I decline friend requests from strangers and acquaintances I only know through business.
Twitter	I use Twitter primarily in *read-only* mode. I follow a diverse group of people to get news, opinions, and insights from different perspectives.
LinkedIn	This is my primary business networking platform. I'm an open networker, and I'm continually looking to expand my connections on LinkedIn. I make an effort to provide interesting content to my LinkedIn connections.
Text messaging	I consider text messaging to be for personal or urgent work matters only. I do not conduct any business with third parties via text.

Social media	Usage
The telephone	Phone calls are important for deeper conversations. Unless it's family, I don't believe in calling someone out of the blue. Phone calls should be scheduled in advance.
Video call	This is quickly replacing the phone call. Adding body language to conversations improves connectivity and understanding between people. Video calls keep us honest since it's harder to multitask when someone is watching. Video calls should be scheduled in advance.
The pub	The original social medium. Don't all good business ideas originate on a bar napkin? There's a good reason for that.

Networking well takes time and commitment. The best networks have been built and nurtured over the years. When cultivating your network, focus on giving rather than taking. Be the George Bailey of networking. Give until it hurts, and when you find yourself in need, your network will be there to take care of you.

In the next chapter, we'll discuss one of the most important aspects of a network: learning from others.

22 Good Advice Doesn't Come Cheap; It's Free

There are many ways for IT professionals to get advice, knowledge, and insights. Books, articles, conferences, consultants, and advisory firms are the most common. I use all these methods to round out my knowledge. You obviously believe in the importance of learning; you're reading a book right now.

Above all of these, the best advice comes from your peer network. Who better to steer you to the best solution than the person who has successfully completed the project you are contemplating?

I work hard to nurture my network. I do this by attending conferences, speaking at events, and following up with the people I meet. Providing useful content is an important aspect of networking.

Even competitors will gain more from collaborating than from secret-keeping. As a CIO, be well-versed in what you should and shouldn't say publicly. Meet with your investor relations team and your public relations team. They will coach you on speaking externally. If you work at a public company, be intimately familiar with your quarterly reports. Mimic what your CEO and CFO have said publicly. This keeps you out of trouble and in lockstep with the company's official position.

"All of us are smarter than any one of us."[29] When we combine our collective knowledge, insights, and experiences, we all grow together.

IV Deliver to Delight: a Collection of Usable Tips and Tools

23

The Written Word—a.k.a. IT Strategy

Susan Barley, one of my mentors, liked to say, "If you didn't write it down, you didn't do it." Does your company have an IT strategy? If you said yes, but you can't produce a document, then you don't have a strategy. Strategies exist on paper, or at least in a PDF, not in the CIO's head. I'm not judging here; in my 20 years as a CIO, at least half the time we didn't have a written IT strategy. According to my LinkedIn poll, only 49 percent of companies have a written IT strategy.

Align Your Strategy

A well-written IT strategy clearly aligns IT's actions with the business objectives. Are you sick of hearing how you need to align IT to the business? So am I. First, IT is part of the business, not outside of it. I recommend that you erase the phrase "IT and the business" from your vocabulary. Instead, say "our partners in the business." Words matter, and how can you expect to be included if you don't include yourself? By using the word *partners*, you establish IT on equal footing across the organization.

Treat the IT strategy as a subset of the business strategy with equal footing to the other strategies, as shown in Figure 23.1.

Figure 23.1: IT Strategy Alignment

What if there is no corporate strategy? If your company doesn't have a written strategy, you need to resolve this before you can move on. Hopefully, that's not the case; however, it does happen. In this situation, you need to document the business strategy before working on the IT strategy. To do this, listen carefully to what your CEO and CFO say internally and externally. There will be themes, and these themes equate to a strategy. If you have a prioritized list of IT and other initiatives, these will also inform the business strategy. For example, if your top projects all involve improving customer experience, that is probably a core element of your business strategy. This creates a terrific opportunity to partner with your CEO. Write down what you see and hear, and discuss it with the CEO. Explain that you're creating an IT strategy, and you want to ensure that IT is properly positioned to help deliver the company's goals.

Create Your Strategy

The authors of the IT strategy should be the IT senior leadership team: usually, the CIO's direct reports. While each member of IT leadership contributes, I recommend that only the CIO update the final document for a consistent voice and tone. An annual offsite of the IT senior leadership team is the perfect venue to create or update the strategy. Align this to the executive team's calendar. If the execs update the company strategy at an annual offsite, simply schedule your meeting a week or two after that one. At the CEO offsite, you'll probably learn a technique or two that you can incorporate into your meeting.

The primary audience for your IT strategy should be the executive leadership team. The detail and content should be written with this group in mind. The secondary audience is every member of your IT team. Everyone rowing the boat needs to understand where the boat is going and the benefit of actually getting there. Other potential audiences include other departments within your company, trusted external partners, and outsiders sent in to evaluate IT. For each audience, create a different version of the document. For global audiences, leave out the cost detail. For executives, leave out the technical details.

The IT strategy should convey who, what, where, when, why, how, and how much. If your strategy is meant to be read, it should be in narrative form. If it's meant to be presented, bullets, charts, and photos work best. Use the corporate strategy as the guide. Remember, this is intended to be a subset of that document, and it should flow seamlessly.

Here are some elements to consider incorporating into your IT strategy:

- Business strategy (restated)
- Executive summary
- Mission, vision, and values for IT
- Organizational chart
- IT "fun facts": number of systems, servers, storage, PCs, help desk tickets, etc.
- Pie chart of operating expense (OPEX) vs. capital expense (CAPEX) that roughly shows the split of maintenance vs. growth
- Graph of IT costs as a percent of revenue over time
- Uptime goals and metrics
- Details of the support model
- App dev approach
- Analytics approach and tools
- Project management methodology
- List of projects mapped back to the business strategy
- S.W.O.T. analysis
- Multi-year roadmap

The written strategy needs to be your best foot forward. Use the company's standard slide templates and style guides. Ask marketing for images you can incorporate into your document. Do not use any slides or photos from the internet. It's inexpensive to purchase slides and stock photos from reputable sources.

If you work for a public company, find the person who does financial reporting. The person who edits the annual report is the person you want to review your document.

Over time, you will develop a library of slides that are board-ready. When your slides are legal, consistent, and professional and follow the corporate template, it's easy to quickly put together a new presentation for the appropriate audience on short notice. Teach this skill to your IT leadership team, and take advantage of cloud storage to share slides among team members.

Put Your Strategy into Action

Once the strategy is complete, it's time to take it on the road. The first stop is the executive conference room. Present the strategy to your executive team, and make final updates based on their input. Next, present it to everyone in IT. Take your time, go through the details, and answer every question. This is the team you're counting on to deliver this strategy, and their full buy-in is required. If something doesn't work, it's not too late to make changes. Step three is everyone else. Ask to speak to departmental leaders across the organization. As mentioned, make a lightweight, non-technical version for these occasions.

Review the strategy each quarter at your IT Department meetings. Leave a copy on your desk in plain view. Use it in your annual reviews, staff meetings, and one-on-ones. Make it a living document, and it will help keep you and your team on course.

While strategy is essential, as discussed in Chapter 11, without the right culture, it's bound to fail. Strategy is just one piece of the puzzle. By combining a winning culture, the right people, and a clear and effective strategy, you will create an unstoppable team. With a strategy in hand, let's get back to the fundamentals and discuss what it takes to run an Amazing IT Department.

24

It's the Uptime, Stupid

In 1992, campaign strategist James Carville coined the phrase, "it's the economy, stupid." At that time, Carville was attempting to emphasize the importance of the struggling economy in then-candidate Bill Clinton's presidential campaign.[30] The economy was in bad shape, and they knew without improving the economy, nothing else mattered. The same goes for IT: "It's the uptime, stupid." As discussed in Chapter 5, Figure 5.1, if you can't keep your systems operational, achieving KTLO, the foundation level of the Laudato Hierarchy of IT Needs, the rest of your efforts are futile.

Somewhere along the way, I realized that IT could do more harm than good. You may have the best systems, processes, and people money can buy, but if your business isn't offering products or services people want, your business will still fail. On the other hand, if your products are amazing but your systems aren't up to the task, your business is on thin ice. In the digital age, hospitals, factories, warehouses, and retail stores can no longer operate without systems and networks. The hotdog cart in Central Park takes Apple Pay, and subway buskers accept donations via Venmo. All businesses are digital businesses.

Every CIO wants a seat at the table. Ensuring that systems are available, performant, and accurate is a critical first step. If you don't keep your emails emailing and your registers ringing, there's no way you're going to be invited to the CEO's office for a coffee chat.

When you do get a seat at the table, be careful not to become the resident audio-visual expert in the room. The moment the projector stops working, everyone in the room will turn to the CIO. You're the techie, so you need to fix the TV. While I'm sure that you know how to fix it (usually it's the Source button), I caution you against fixing it. It's hard to have a seat at the table when you're under the table. There is nothing executive about tracing HDMI cables or downloading drivers. I'm an advocate of rolling up my sleeves and working side-by-side with the team, but not at a board meeting. To avoid this, I always station an end-user technician outside the room for critical meetings. When you're asked to fix the projector, say sure, and summon the tech. When the board meeting is offsite, congrats: the tech will get to spend the day at a five-star hotel. Have the tech bring a supply of charging cables for every model of phone and laptop, so when someone needs one, it's there for the taking.

Measuring Uptime

Uptime is important, so you need to measure it. The first step in the process is to negotiate service-level objectives (SLOs) with your business partners. I prefer the term *objectives* instead of *agreements* internally. Service-level agreements (SLAs) are contractual obligations between a company and its service providers. Internally, we all work for the same company, and avoiding legal constructs feels more collaborative. When establishing SLOs, take into account the need for planned downtime. While your business partners don't ever want their systems to be down, they would much rather know in advance than be surprised. If you need to patch the servers once a month, schedule this in advance and negotiate a time that works best for your business.

Some systems require 24/7/365 availability. Hospitals, nuclear power plants, and Netflix all fall into this category. Just be aware that *always up* is much more expensive than *almost always up*. Establishing and publishing SLOs allows CIOs to match their infrastructure to the business need. Do you believe moving everything to the cloud solves your uptime issues? Think again. In 2020, Amazon, Google, IBM, Microsoft, and Oracle all had major outages.

AN EXAMPLE OF ESTABLISHING AND REPORTING ON AN SLO

The CIO meets with the chief supply chain officer, and they agree the warehouse management system (WMS) will be available 23 hours/day with a daily maintenance window between 4:00 a.m. and 5:00 a.m. local time. The planned minutes are 23 hours × 60 minutes per hour = 1,380 minutes. If there are no outages outside of the planned window, the uptime is 100%. If the maintenance runs long and the system doesn't come back up until 6:30 a.m., we have an unplanned outage of 90 minutes. In this example: 1,290 actual minutes / 1,380 planned minutes = 93.5% uptime. Note that uptime during the planned outage window does not count. If maintenance is running late and the WMS is down from 4:30 a.m. to 5:30 a.m., this is a 30-minute outage.

What's a good goal for uptime? The longer the time over which you spread your calculation, the easier the math becomes. Watch out for this trick from your vendors. In a 30-day month, this WMS system has 41,400 planned minutes of uptime. With a 99% uptime goal, you can be down almost 7 hours and still meet your SLO goal. A fair goal for an established system is 99.9% uptime per month. In this example, it allows for 41 minutes of unplanned downtime. The term *five 9s*, popular with the Six Sigma crowd, means your uptime is 99.999%. If five 9s is your goal, only 30 seconds of downtime will be acceptable per month.

Establish SLOs for all of your key systems, agree on an acceptable percent uptime, and make uptime a key performance metric for everyone in IT.

Nuances of Measuring Uptime

Should you measure, report, and hold your people accountable for software-as-a-service (SaaS) uptime? It's a complex debate. On the one hand, you have no control over their processes or technology stack. On the other hand, if you aren't responsible, who is? Your CEO? Your CFO? Nobody?

If your SaaS provider is down, it needs to be on the CIO. If CIOs abdicate responsibility for cloud and SaaS systems, what's the point of the CIO? CIOs negotiate the SLAs with the third parties, and CIOs should be actively involved in the recovery of SaaS apps. If it's a small provider, you should be in contact with the principals to ensure that your system takes priority over other customers. After the incident is resolved, meet with the provider to review what happened, and hold them accountable to make improvements. For larger providers, focus your attention on how the system was set up and configured. Your team may not have selected the most redundant or reliable option available during the initial setup.

What if the systems are up but the LAN is down? If the end-user can't access the system, it counts as an outage. If the system is up but inaccurate, that counts as an outage.

Measure report availably in a binary fashion. Daily reports should have an established delivery time. If sales reports are due at 6:00 a.m., they either made it or they didn't. Each day you missed counts against uptime. Being on time 29 of 30 days scores 96.6 percent. As with systems, if your report comes out on time but the data is inaccurate, your score is zero for that day.

Other edge cases can make uptime reporting complicated. If a system is up but has reduced capability or slow response time, I'll ask my business partner to select the impact. In the WMS example, if the system response time led to 30 minutes of extra work, I let the business owner decide how much to dock from the uptime calculation. They can pick 30 minutes or the entire day; it's their call.

Information Technology Infrastructure Library (ITIL)

Pronounced "eye-till," ITIL is short for Information Technology Infrastructure Library. ITIL is a model that provides for implementing IT service management (ITSM) across all IT domains. ITSM software, including ServiceNow and EasyVista, is designed around ITIL workflows. I can't go deeper into this subject without boring you to death, but I encourage you to spend time exploring ITIL principles. ITIL is free, and it can be used as a framework to build your processes for incident management, problem management, and other IT services. ITIL is customer-centric, and it emphasizes getting to the root cause of problems. For more on ITIL, check out https://www.itlibrary.org/.

When You Have a Problem, Proclaim It Loudly

My CEO loves calling me when we're having system problems. She's highly attuned to what is going on in our business. There's little that makes me unhappier than hearing about a problem from Sharon *before*

I hear about it from my team. Our goal is perfection; when that is not achieved, the next most important task is promptly notifying our business partners and providing regular status updates. Whether it's the CEO or an intern, it's IT's job to detect issues and notify our partners before they notify us.

The best way to accomplish this is to develop and follow a formal incident reporting process. ITIL provides guidelines for creating this process. Create the process in advance, set up the notification groups, and train your IT team on the process so it is executed properly every time. ITIL recommends using a matrix that evaluates both impact and urgency to determine the severity of an outage. This is overkill. When is a major system outage not urgent? Use impact to create your severity levels. See Figure 24.1 for a sample incident reporting process.

Incident level	Definition	Notification group	Notification method	Notification frequency
Severity 1	-Broad impact -Work stoppage -Revenue stream down	-All of IT, business leaders across the org	-Email and text message. Confirm message was received by IT leadership. -CIO calls CEO.	-Every hour until resolved
Severity 2	-Affecting multiple users or locations -Cumbersome or no workaround	-IT incident group -Affected IT and business leaders	-Email message	-Every two hours until resolved
Severity 3	-Smaller incident, workaround in place	-IT incident group -Affected IT and business leaders	-Email message	-Every four hours until resolved

Figure 24.1: Sample ITIL Incident Reporting Process

Troubleshooting

Most IT problems take around five minutes to fix. Unfortunately, it could take hours to determine what the problem is and even longer to find the person with the skills to do that. A structured troubleshooting process will reduce these lead times. When something goes awry, follow these steps:

1. Notify your business partners.
2. Gather the right people.

3. Appoint a "Storm Boss."
4. Appoint a comms person.
5. Open a technical conference call.
6. When the issue is resolved, hold a retrospective.

In today's world, most outages involve a third-party provider. You should have a list of key contacts and escalation points for all of your key vendors. Don't hesitate to call the highest-ranking person you know at the provider. Don't underestimate the power of salespeople in these scenarios. They are skilled connectors, and they know who's who in their organization.

Storm Boss is the person you put in charge of troubleshooting. The head of infrastructure or operations is ideal in this role. If it's a security-related incident, the CISO should be the Storm Boss. The Storm Boss is the decision-maker.

The best role for the CIO during a major outage is communications. Don't let your business partners on the technical conference call. Obsessed with transparency, I once thought this was a good idea. It backfired. You don't want your head of store operations or your warehouse manager talking directly to your engineers in the middle of a firefight. No need to elaborate further—the reasons for this are obvious.

The most likely cause of an incident is recent changes. The most cringe-worthy thing you'll hear in a change management meeting is, "This change will have no impact." Call me superstitious, but teasing the IT gods is ill-advised, and a major outage is likely in your future.

When I learned to fly an airplane, the instructor drilled into me that when something goes wrong, undo the last thing you did. If you pull the mixture knob and the engine goes dead, push it back in. When users suddenly have trouble accessing apps, consider the firewall rules you just implemented the most likely culprit. If you use feature toggles, toggle any new features off and see if this resolves the problem.

I once worked for a boss, who will go unnamed, who wanted to know who was to blame in the middle of an outage. This is not the time to assign blame or dole out punishments. When the fire is still burning, focus 100 percent on fire fighting. After the problem is resolved, hold a retrospective. Learn from the incident so that it doesn't happen again. Don't punish your team for mistakes during or after an incident—turn mistakes into valuable learning experiences.

Let Them Eat Cake

If you're in the middle of a major outage, make sure your behavior is appropriate. A somber, humble demeanor is expected in these scenarios. Even if you aren't involved in the troubleshooting, joking, laughing, or heading out for an early happy hour is tone-deaf behavior. Cancel your dinner plans and stay at the office until the systems are operational again.

Change Management

Mature IT organizations have a change advisory board (CAB) that reviews and approves all changes. ITIL provides details on how to set up and run these meetings. I integrate the CAB meeting into the daily IT meeting that I discuss in detail in the next section. At The Vitamin Shoppe, we discuss IT changes with over 100 people daily. Everyone is well abreast of upcoming changes.

What constitutes a change? It's not just deploying new software. Operating system upgrades, patches, hotfixes, configuration changes, low-code/no-code deployments, and data fixes are all production changes, and they need to be reviewed and approved by the CAB before they move to production. If the change worked during testing, there's still a possibility it won't work in production. If you didn't test your change, it's guaranteed not to work in production. These are not only best practices; change management is a common Sarbanes-Oxley (SOX) control.

Daily Meeting

Communication is a critical component of leadership. With all or part of a team working remotely, intentional communication is even more necessary. For over 20 years and at three different companies, I've run a daily IT meeting to review incidents and discuss upcoming changes. For the first 20 years, this meeting included all of IT management. When the pandemic hit in 2020, the meeting moved to a video conference, allowing us to enlarge the invitation list. We expanded the meeting to include a sales update, an inventory update, a supply chain update, and even a health and wellness update. At The Vitamin Shoppe, every corporate office employee is invited to the meeting, and we average over 100 virtual attendees every single day. I am pleased and proud that our entire executive team regularly attends, including our CEO, Sharon Leite. This is a quick meeting, lasting no more than 15 minutes. It has been one of the tools we use to keep our culture strong while working remotely. Even when we go back to the office, we will keep the meeting open to all. Incidents and problems are openly discussed, changes are announced before they are deployed, and successes and milestones are celebrated on this call. Mike Provost, our emcee, expertly manages the flow of the call, keeping it crisp and fun. The chat feature in Microsoft Teams is a bonus, allowing participants to add information during the call.

Annual Readiness

Many businesses have a peak season. Retailers have a huge spike in sales at the end of the year. The peak day for pizza delivery is Super Bowl Sunday. Before the cloud gave us elastic capacity, we had to build our systems to handle the biggest day of the year. "Build the church for Easter Sunday" was the mantra. To prepare for the peak, CIOs established a peak-season readiness program. This includes technical tasks like capacity planning, stress testing, and performance enhancements. Peak-season planning also includes updating vendor and employee contact lists, creating a coverage schedule, and possibly setting up a war room for the biggest days. Most IT shops freeze production deployments during peak season because, as we know, changes cause incidents.

Some companies are less seasonal, or they have unpredictable peak sales days. Did Kylie Jenner just recommend your product on Instagram? Buckle up, because here comes your biggest sales day of the year. If you don't have a peak season, odds are you don't have a peak-season planning program. When was the last time you updated your contact list for your key partners? Take a page from the seasonal business and implement an annual readiness program for your steady business.

25 If It's Important, You Better Get Two

Whether it's a server, a router, or a business analyst, if your business relies on it, you need to have more than one. There are many gotchas in redundancy. Let's review some of the more significant ones:

- *Each individual node needs to operate below 50% capacity.* If the workload on each device is over 50%, and one fails, the remaining node will be overtaxed, and it will fail as well. This is a tricky problem. As server load slowly moves from 40 to 50 to 60% utilized, it's still a happy server, and no alerts or warnings are produced. However, the moment node A fails, the 60% load on node B becomes 120%, and now you have an outage. If you convinced your CFO to invest in redundancy, and this happens, you've got some explaining to do. The moment your utilization crosses 50%, you no longer have redundancy. To avoid this scenario, set your alerts at 45%: 45% utilized is actually 90% utilized, and therefore it's time to add capacity.

- *Two of everything costs twice as much, or more, than one of everything.* If one 10 gig internet circuit costs $5,000/month, guess how much two 10 gig internet circuits cost? If you said $10,000, you got it right. And remember, we need to run these circuits at less than 50% utilization, so redundant internet circuits double your costs with no additional capacity. The story gets worse. To manage two circuits, you need two network switches, two VPN concentrators, two firewalls, and dual power. You need private IP space, and you need all of it properly configured so when one circuit fails, there is no business impact. Redundancy doesn't come cheaply. If your goal is 100% uptime with no planned outages, it's going to get even more expensive.

- Ensure that your redundancy doesn't hide system failures. Here's a painful, true story that's happened to me more than once. I'm on my way to a meeting when a buzz starts to fill the office. Someone shouts, "The internet is down!" Of course, I'm doubtful the actual internet is down, but I get the point. The company's access to the internet is down, and work has come to a halt. The incident team is activated, the messages go out, and the trouble-shooting begins. The carrier is having a global outage affecting more than one customer. It happens, but we've spent time, money, and energy ensuring that we have a fully functioning redundant circuit. So why are we down? It turns out the "other" circuit failed a few weeks ago, and nobody noticed. The redundancy worked too well. When the first failure occurred, business carried on as usual. This was fine until the second circuit failed, and now both circuits are down. Most companies have alerting in place, but is anybody listening? Does your network manager get so many alerts that they're ignored? Are the alerts going to a person who no longer works at your company? As with the capacity problem, investing in redundancy and having it still fail is worse than no redundancy at all.

- *Be wary of the weakest link in your redundancy.* If the server is dual powered and both plugs are plugged into the same power leg, you have a single point of failure. If two redundant network switches are stacked in the same rack, and that rack has an electrical fire, you have a single point of failure. I once lost both internet circuits in a distribution center when a truck hit a utility pole. The reason: both of my internet carriers had fiber on that pole. When designing your redundant network, look for physical and logical diversity. When you see them digging in the streets around your office, just know that the backhoe operator is intent on ruining your day.

- *Active/passive redundancy won't work when you need it.* The most effective redundancy is called active/active, and it means that all the nodes are always operating and performing tasks. In *active/passive*, a backup or standby node is waiting to take over when the primary node fails. The reason it doesn't work well is that the passive node becomes neglected. We had a big snow-storm in the Northeast recently, and out came the snowblowers.

Many hadn't been started since last winter, and they didn't work when they were needed. I'm confident every owner had plans to run their snowblower at least once a month all summer or to drain the fuel and store it away properly. But we all get busy, and secondary tasks like maintaining a snowblower or a backup server get forgotten.

■ *Redundant systems need to be stateless.* When a request comes in, any server needs to be able to process that request. If applications are holding state, load-balancing doesn't work. We built stateless apps back in the IBM mainframe days because we had limited computing resources. This practice got lost during the fat-client era. Fortunately, *stateless* is in vogue again as applications have moved to the cloud. For more on this, I recommend the free e-book *Beyond the Twelve-Factor App* by Kevin Hoffman.[31]

Redundancy and Probability Math

An old big-iron guy myself, I've always known that mainframes are more reliable than commodity servers. Mainframes use more reliable components, manage heat more effectively, and have redundancy built into the chassis and the logic. However, a bit of probability math changed my stance on using commodity hardware versus mainframes. If you have two or more independent and redundant servers, the odds of them both failing at the same time is calculated by multiplying the failures rates. Let's compare a mainframe with a 99.99% uptime to a cluster of two low-end servers:

■ Mainframe uptime: 99.99%.
■ Cheap server uptime: 98%.
■ The failure rate for servers is 2% or 0.02.
■ Probability of a concurrent double failure = $0.02 \times 0.02 = 0.0004$.

Two low-end servers provide *99.96%* uptime: almost as good as the expensive mainframe for a fraction of the cost.

Now let's add one more server into the mix:

■ Probability of triple failure = $0.02 \times 0.02 \times 0.02 = 0.000008$.

Three low-end servers provide an uptime of *99.9992!*

Does your business require the highest level of redundancy at any cost? Chain together two or three mainframes, and watch how many nines follow the decimal point now.

The Only True Test

Are you proud of your redundancy? If you are, walk into your data center and turn something off. Just pick one of those big boxes with blinking lights and a loud fan, locate the power switch, and shut it off. I'm joking—don't do this. But to truly validate your redundancy, you need to test it. Plan a test, communicate it well, and shut down servers, switches, load-balancers, circuits, and power distribution units. If you run passive redundancy, fail over to the backup. If this test goes poorly, you need to do it more frequently. Like exercise, redundancy is a use-it-or-lose-it proposition. If you get into a habit of running this test every month, your redundancy will be there for you when you need it.

Does Any of This Matter in the Cloud?

You may wonder why I've written so much about servers and switches when everything is moving to the cloud. Because actually, it isn't. "End-user spending on global data center infrastructure is projected to reach $200 billion in 2021, an increase of 6% from 2020, according to the latest forecast from Gartner, Inc."[32] I predict that large companies will keep a hybrid environment for the foreseeable future. Some will even move workload back to their own data centers to better manage costs. We need to remind ourselves that "the cloud" is simply computers in someone else's data center. Regardless of the cloud provider, the responsibility of managing redundancy, security, performance, and cost still sits with the CIO.

All machines eventually break, and all humans make mistakes. Properly managed and configured redundancy allows us to keep our business running even when these things occur.

In the next chapter, we'll talk about the most important aspect of managing systems: cyber-security.

26 Lock It Down

The first rule of cyber-security is, you don't talk about cyber-security. *Fight Club* jokes aside, cyber-security is a huge topic. Entire books are written about it, and none of them can comprehensively cover every aspect. This isn't a security book, but we will stop for a moment to reflect on a few core concepts.

Keeping your data and systems secure is paramount and needs to be a primary consideration for every IT project and process. CISOs talk about the CIA triad. Not the CIA you're thinking of; in this context, CIA stands for confidentiality, integrity, and availability. A mature cyber-security program seeks to keep data private, reliable, and available to those, and only those, who need it.

Cyber-attacks and ransomware can be devastating to a company. A comprehensive cyber-security program should be risk-based, follow a framework (such as NIST, HiTrust, CIS, ISO 27001, or COBIT),[33] and measure and report key metrics. In a public company, I recommend that the CIO and CISO provide a cyber-security update to the audit committee every quarter and an annual presentation to the full board. Here are five key principles:

- If you don't need the data, don't keep the data.
- Follow the *least privilege principle*: only provide the minimum access required.
- Segment and lock down your network. Lock the outside doors and the inside doors.
- Require multi-factor authentication for remote access.
- Educate your end-users: phishing is still a top attack vector.

In most companies, the CIO is responsible for all applicable IT audits. Audits vary by industry. Some audits are government-mandated, and some are industry self-regulation, including the PCI-DSS, which is required to accept credit cards. Audits are also mandated by banks and insurance companies as a requirement for loans and insurance, respectively. Public companies must pass an annual IT controls audit as part of Sarbanes-Oxley (SOX). It's important to understand that passing an audit doesn't mean your environment is secure, and establishing a secure environment doesn't mean you'll pass an audit. For example, SOX is only concerned with financial reporting, limiting which applications are in scope for the audit. CIOs and CISOs need to secure all of their systems. The bad actors will look for the weakest link. On the flip side, auditors require written documentation that, while important, is not relevant to the environment's security. The lesson here is to, first and foremost, focus your efforts on creating a robust program to secure your network. Document as you go so when the auditors show up, you'll not only be secure, but you'll also be able to prove it.

All of this is part of keeping the lights on (KTLO) in the Laudato Hierarchy of IT Needs pyramid (see Chapter 5, Figure 5.1, The Laudato Hierarchy of IT Needs). Once the environment is reliable and secure, the IT Department can take the next step up the pyramid and focus on becoming lean and efficient.

27 Lean and Efficient IT

Get it right, then get it cheap. The second level of the Laudato Hierarchy of IT Needs is lean and efficient IT (see Chapter 5, Figure 5.1, Laudato Hierarchy of IT Needs). With reliable systems and mature processes, we can turn our focus to reducing IT costs. To do an expert job of cost-cutting, you're going to have to dig more deeply into the details. Have your IT finance partner provide you with a spreadsheet of every vendor you've paid and how much you've paid them in the past 18 months. Sort your list in descending order, and focus on the largest suppliers first.

Now you need to go digging for IT software and services that don't roll up to the IT budget. This is affectionately known as *shadow IT*. Marketing and Human Resources are always good places to look for shadow IT. In this step, some accounting knowledge will be useful. Software outside of IT will be charged to a different department (sometimes called a *unit*) in the general ledger (GL) but most likely the same account numbers you see in your IT budget. Ask your IT finance partner to extract all vendors and payments to those accounts across every department. Note: be sure to get permission from the department head and the CFO before you start rooting around in someone else's GL. The next method for identifying shadow IT is to ask your support team. Your business partners may demo software, implement software, manage the access, and pay the bill, but they're still calling IT when the software has an issue. Once you've identified the shadow IT costs, add them to your spreadsheet and re-sort.

Next up, get a copy of the contracts for each of the vendors you're paying. Some of these agreements will predate your tenure, possibly by a long time. If you can't find a contract, check with the legal department, your sourcing department, the executive assistants, and your resident packrat. Every organization has that one person who holds onto everything. If you still have no contract, that's a sticky situation. Either you're doing business without a contract, or it's lost. Tread lightly here; you don't want to call up Oracle and say, "Hey, I lost our contract; can you send a copy over?"

Software

The first area to explore for savings opportunities is software. Software includes IT-specific tools, productivity tools, and enterprise business software. Follow this mantra: eliminate, consolidate, negotiate. Do you still need the tool? If not, cancel the contract and reap all the savings. If you still need it, is there an opportunity to consolidate? You may be paying for tools that are now included with your Microsoft or Google productivity bundle. Do you have Teams and Zoom? Do you have Teams and Slack? Do you have Teams and Box? Zoom, Slack, and Box are all terrific products, but are they really necessary add-ons in your situation? Education goes a long way in this process. Microsoft Visio is $15/user/month. It's common for users to request Visio when they only require the free Visio viewer. Make sure you fully understand the features of the tools you already own before you buy or keep another add-on product.

Understand your metrics and your contract. If you pay per user / per month, true up the user counts every month and only pay for what you need. If you're deep into cost-cutting, it may be because your business is experiencing a downturn. If you're using fewer services, be sure to only pay for fewer services.

Read and re-read those contracts. I once found a gem in a legacy support contract from the 1990s. In a threatening manner, this clause stated, "If you drop support, you'll be required to pay for actual support hours used at $200/hour." Since we only called this vendor two or three times each year, the once expensive-sounding hourly rate was a bargain compared to the annual maintenance fees we were paying. Can you move from platinum support to gold support? It's usually an option; weigh the pros and the cons, and make a business decision. If it's a smaller vendor, move to a lower support model and build a business relationship with the VP of support. You'll get much better service through the relationship than you ever did through the contract.

If your situation is more desperate, riskier options can reduce costs even further. You may choose to move to third-party support or go self-supported. Third-party support advocates claim they're both cheaper and better—but do your own research. If you head down either path, first get full buy-in from your executive partners. Carefully document the decision so you aren't being admonished in perpetuity by your successors.

Take all of these steps before you negotiate. A deep discount on something you don't need is still a waste of money. Once you've eliminated unneeded software, consolidated duplicate software, and right-sized support, it's finally time to negotiate a better price for the software you're keeping. At this stage, my recommendation is to get help from a professional. Either partner with your internal strategic sourcing team or hire a third party to negotiate on your behalf.

It's not hard to find a company that will negotiate software agreements on a commission basis. You pay a percentage of the savings. CIOs are superheroes, and we like to do it all ourselves; however, some jobs call for a full-time professional. Plumbing, brain surgery, and software negotiation are three good examples.

Legality

You may not like what you find when you dig into the details. It's possible you'll discover that you're using something you're not licensed for, or you're using a free version intended for personal use in a business setting. The freeware version of some software may be legal to use but not ideal for data privacy and security. If you do find something concerning, don't panic. Partner with your CFO and your chief counsel to immediately rectify the situation. Paying for more than you are using is a waste of money—and using more than you pay for is unethical and illegal. To reduce risk, consider implementing a software asset management (SAM) tool. These are usually add-on modules to IT service management (ITSM) software.

Cloud Services

The biggest cloud misnomer is that you only pay for what you use. This is not true; you actually pay for what you configure plus what you use. If you have an idle server in your data center, the only cost to you is electricity and air conditioning. However, if you configure the same server in a public cloud, you're going to be charged a monthly fee whether you use it or not.

Here's a cautionary tale that might be based on a true story. A bad piece of code gets deployed to production and gobbles up CPU and memory. It's out of control, and soon it crashes your in-house server. Whether virtualized or not, no financial harm is done; the offending code is removed, the server is rebooted, and the developer heads back to the drawing board. In the cloud, this could get ugly. Google, AWS, and Azure all have automatic scaling. Capacity-on-demand is one of the primary benefits of the cloud. But if your rogue process runs in this environment, it could rack up a sizeable bill. Amazon even brags that you only pay for what you use (how kind of them):

> *There are no additional fees with Amazon EC2 Auto Scaling, so it's easy to try it out and see how it can benefit your AWS architecture. You only pay for the AWS resources that you use.*[34]
>
> *Amazon EC2 Auto Scaling User Guide*

At the very least, don't set test and QA servers to auto-scale. I was a developer once. I've yet to meet a server that I couldn't cripple with some poorly written code.

Properly controlling cloud costs requires new technical and business knowledge. Does your workload run more cost-effectively on four small virtual servers or one large virtual server? When it's well managed, the variability capacity of the cloud will help optimize IT spending. If you let your cloud run wild, your costs will soon follow.

Telcom

If you're a company with hundreds or thousands of locations, telecommunications costs represent a large percentage of your IT spend. Phone lines, data circuits, and wireless plans all add up at scale. This is such a messy business that an entire industry has sprung up around managing these costs. I once had a conversation with a major telecommunications company executive (his card said VP, but who knows) and inquired why the company couldn't produce an accurate bill. His argument was incompetence. He claimed that a series of mergers combined with crushing regulations was just too much for the billing systems. The problem I have with this argument is that the bill always seems to be wrong in the company's favor. While nobody should be proud of proclaiming incompetence, if it was truly a broken system, shouldn't it sometimes be wrong in our favor? I'm not making accusations here; just something to ponder.

Regardless of the reason why, billion-dollar businesses now exist to resell telecommunication services. These businesses promise and deliver better service, lower costs, and accurate and transparent billing. While the major telcos require recurring monthly, annual, and term commitments, resellers will agree to a pay-as-you-go model. Most of these resellers bundle support of your network and your network equipment, providing a turnkey solution. If you go this route, insist on a la carte pricing. Bundling is a favorite technique to hide margin. Technology and business needs change rapidly, so retain the ability to add and drop services, even in a single-provider arrangement.

This industry is saturated with providers, and they employ the most aggressive sales tactics I've seen. My advice is to use your CIO network to find the best partner and to be wary of the group that's stalking your CEO and your board.

Professional Services

If you take just one point from this book, it's that *people aren't fungible*. If you think you can save money by going with the lowest-cost consultant, contractor, and offshore team, think again. Earlier, we discussed tactics for getting the most value from third-party consultants. One of the benefits of using external resources is the ease of letting them go. Always put a *term for convenience clause* in your consulting contracts to retain this flexibility. If you need to cut costs in a hurry, start with external resources.

When renegotiating rates with incumbent providers, consider using a volume rebate. Most companies will provide volume discounts when you make a long-term commitment. However, long-term commitments take away your flexibility. Enter the rebate. A rebate provides for a discount once certain volume levels are obtained—the best of both worlds for you and the provider.

A less obvious cost reduction tactic is to hire your consultants. Generally, the fully loaded cost of an employee is less than the hourly rate. Converting consultants to employees improves morale while saving costs. The downside is you lose the flexibility consultants provide, and you may be putting yourself at risk of having to lay off these employees when additional cost-cutting is required.

Capital Expenses Drive Operating Expenses

If you've been directed to cut your IT operating expenses, you need to push back on the project spending. In organizations focused on EBITDA (earnings before interest, taxes, depreciation, and amortization), there tends to be more concern over the operating expenses than the capital expenses because capital is excluded from EBITDA. CIOs need to make it clear that even capital projects drive up operating costs. To reduce IT spending, you need to reduce the project load.

The Small Stuff

Does your internal help desk have a 1-800 number? Why is that? Long-distance calling is now included with every phone plan. The 1-800 number could be costing you $10,000 or $20,000 or $30,000 per year for no good reason. Small charges like these will never cross your desk, but they add up.

One way to find these hidden costs is to sign every single invoice for a set period of time. When you review every invoice, you'll learn a lot about your department, and you'll find that you're paying for things you weren't aware of. Ask your AP manager to set you as a required approver for every invoice in your department. Be very clear with your team about why you're doing this; you don't want to come across as a micromanager. Be available to sign every day so you don't become a bottleneck. When I did this at Pier 1 Imports, a few things really surprised me. Every month we received one or two invoices from a locksmith for safe cracking. These ran around $300 each. When the store manager lost the keys to the store safe, they called the IT help desk to dispatch a locksmith. Who knew? Not a huge expense, but when you're benchmarked, you need to be sure only IT costs are in your numbers. Another issue I uncovered were bills for printer cartridges that came from scammers. The scammer would call the store and ask what printer model they had. They would then ship cartridges to that store and send us a bill for the printer cartridge at a ridiculous markup. The scammer would use the store's acceptance of the package as their "proof" of receipt and demand payment. We worked with our legal department to tell these scammers to "go away," and we worked with store operations to educate the stores not to fall for these deceptive tactics. When you sign every invoice, you learn a lot about your team. Who pays their bills on time? Who negotiates the best? Digging deeply into every dollar spent will put you in the best position to find opportunities to cut costs in your shop.

Reduction in Force

While each of us is considered a variable cost, a reduction in force (RIF) should only be considered as a last-resort cost-cutting tactic. I recommend you explore every nook and cranny to find savings before you let a single employee go. A layoff severely damages your morale and your reputation, and it takes months, or even years, to recover. How well you execute the RIF will impact your remaining employees. Make every effort to do it professionally. Here are some guidelines:

- Get all the savings you need in a single round. If you have multiple RIFs in a short time, you will never recover, and your remaining employees will all look to jump ship before they're next on the list.
- Keep the RIF confidential during planning. Loose lips sink ships. Leaks are devastating to morale. The rumors are always worse than the truth.
- Treat people with dignity and respect. Keep their confidentiality, pay a fair severance, and do your part to help them find their next opportunity.
- Don't just reduce individual contributors. All levels need to be considered. Increasing span-of-control for yourself and your management team needs to be considered.
- Be visible. As an executive, you need to keep your door open, walk the halls, and eat lunch in the cafeteria. Don't hide in the corner or work remotely on the days after a RIF.

Sometimes a RIF is necessary or worsened due to mistakes you've made in the past. Here are some things you should do to reduce the need or severity of a RIF:

- Deal with poor performers through performance management on an ongoing basis. If you're carrying poor performers on the payroll, you are not maximizing value for your organization, and this will eventually backfire.
- Don't get too bloated during the good times. Plan your resource requirements over a three-year horizon. Staff to the valleys, not the peaks. Use temp labor to fill in the rest.
- Aggressively manage all the other IT costs. Laying off an employee to cover rising software costs is backward.

Less Is More

The simpler your IT stack, the more stable and cost-effective it will be. Minimize complexity, and you'll be well-positioned to move up the Laudato Hierarchy of IT Needs pyramid. Throughout the chapters in the rest of this part of the book, we'll look at techniques and approaches you can use to create value, which will, in turn, free you up to better innovate.

28 What Should I Work on First?

Around 10 years ago, I was at a CIO networking event, and there was a newly minted CIO in the room. He was new to his company and new to the role of CIO. Before we were even seated for dinner, someone casually asked the new CIO what he was working on. His answer made us cringe: "Oh, everything. It's a mess. We need a new ERP, a new POS, new marketing tools, and on and on." A grizzled and well-respected CIO confidently replied, "You shouldn't do any of that in your first year. It's too much to take on when you're new." The veteran CIO continued, "When it goes wrong, they're going to blame you." The new CIO was incredulous and asked, "Well then, what should I do first?" The answer made me laugh and changed my perspective forever: "You should get your executives Blackberries."

We've already explored the role IT has in delivering value to an organization. To succeed in creating value, we need to build credibility, limit how much we take on at once, and properly sequence projects so that logical prerequisites are completed first. Today's equivalent to "getting executives Blackberries" is creating value with low-risk, high reward projects. Prioritizing a project that benefits the executive team or your new business partners is ideal; this will help you establish essential relationships and build trust.

Use the matrix shown in Figure 28.1 to evaluate projects.

Figure 28.1: Project Prioritization Evaluation Matrix

If a project has low reward and low risk, that means it's small and potentially meaningless. I found that individual contributors love working on these types of projects, because they can quickly solve problems for the internal customers. Fix a report heading, and Jessie in accounting will bake cookies for you. I love cookies, but prioritizing the little things at the expense of the more impactful projects does not create meaningful value for your company.

I'm not suggesting that the small things should be ignored. The two approaches that work best are to (i) bundle several small enhancements into a large project so that combined, they have a larger reward; or (ii) bundle them into larger projects. Sometimes I call these small items *sand* in reference to the story of the rock, pebbles, and sand. The *classic rock, pebbles, and sand* story is commonly told as a lesson in time management, and it works nicely as a metaphor for completing IT work as well. Fill a jar up to the top with rocks, and it appears full. However, if you pour in some pebbles, there is room in the spaces, and they all fit inside the jar that appeared full with just the larger rocks inside. With both rocks and pebbles in the jar, now it really appears full. The final step is to add sand to the jar. The jar we twice believed was full can also hold sand since spaces remain between the rocks and the pebbles.

Usually, large IT projects have the capacity to take on medium and smaller changes. When you're working on the big rocks, throw some pebbles and sand in there, too. To keep our analogy going, remember, at no point did we overfill the jar. Only add medium and small tasks to your project if they can be accomplished without affecting the time and the budget.

Have you identified projects with a high reward and low risk? Do these first. The most obvious example is analytics projects. New reports, dashboards, balanced scorecards, and machine learning analysis will provide immediate benefits without any risk. Ask your business partners what information would help them run their business better and deliver results. Another lower-risk initiative is to improve sub-optimal processes. If it's already not working well, the odds are you won't make it worse.

What about high-risk, low-reward initiatives? My prime example would be a payroll system. No system gets audited more than payroll. At least every other Friday, your payroll system is being audited, and it better balance to the penny. There are legal and morale issues if employees aren't paid accurately and on time, every time. My advice:

outsource payroll. There's no competitive advantage to having the world's best payroll system. Outsource this to the experts so you can keep your team focused on higher-reward efforts.

Ultimately, successfully completing the high-risk, high-reward projects is how IT delivers maximum value to the company. As much as possible, mitigate these efforts to keep the risk as low as possible. Building prototypes, expanded testing, and incremental delivery are all effective techniques to reduce risk. When you're a new CIO, stay in the low-risk, high-reward quadrant until you have enough credibility to take on the really hard stuff.

29 Limit Your Work in Process (WIP)

Here's a rhetorical question: Do you want to get more done? The answer is yes, of course. We're all racing to embrace digital, and digital capabilities are the only hope for many companies' survival. To maximize output, you need to do fewer things at a time. Embrace this mantra:

Stop Starting and Start Finishing

Don't confuse activity with delivery. It's a mistake to kick off the next project before you've completed any of the items already in the hopper. Get something done before you move on.

I recommend setting a work in process (WIP) limit for your project portfolio. Count how many projects you have in flight, and set the new limit 10–20 percent below that. For example, if you have 17 projects underway, set your WIP limit at 14 or 15. If you have 100 in-flight projects, then dropping all the way down to 80 may make sense. Use your best judgment here—as long as you end up with fewer in-flight projects, you're going to increase your throughput.

Don't start a new project until you fall below your WIP limit. When a project completes, assign the newly available resources to the highest-ranked project possible. Putting more resources on your top-ranked projects will reduce their duration and get you to value sooner. Starting a new project does the opposite; it moves resources to your lowest-ranked and, therefore, least-important project.

The principle of establishing a WIP limit comes from Lean, and the Agile community has adopted it. If you want to explore these concepts more deeply, read up on Lean[13], Little's Law[35], and Kanban[36].

Of course, simply limiting the number of projects you're working on doesn't help a lot unless you know how to prioritize them. The next chapter examines a technique for doing precisely that.

30 One List to Rule Them All

It's quiz time again: what's the #1 IT project in your company? I'm sure you got that right. Now they get a bit harder: what's the #7 IT project in your company? #10, #15, #25? You're only able to answer these questions if you have a ranked priority list.

Having a written, ranked priority list for all IT projects creates both clarity and alignment. By aligning your efforts toward the #1 project, you significantly improve the chances of succeeding with the work the company has deemed most important. When a person frees up, instead of starting the next project, apply them to the highest-ranked project. This is known as *swarming*. When assigning staff to projects, put your best and brightest on the top projects. Doing so creates opportunities for your stars, and it further improves your chances of success. As a CIO, your time to attend meetings is limited. Use the ranked list to decide where to spend your time. If a project isn't on the list, don't unintentionally sanction it by attending a discussion or vendor demo on the topic.

A lot of organizations rank priorities. A great example is college football. There are 130 teams in the Division I college Football Bowl Subdivision (FBS). Only four of these teams make it to the playoffs each year. College football uses a ranking system to determine the best teams. This is not unlike your project list. It's easy to get a list of 130 or more items, even in a medium-sized IT Department. An enlightening and fun exercise is to have your executive team independently rank your projects from 1 to 25 the same way college coaches rank teams.

Create Your List

The first step is to list the top 30 or so projects. I'm not talking about your must-do projects, like mandatory upgrades; I'm talking about value-creating ROI projects. We'll get to the "required" projects later.

If you don't have a list, or you have several lists, the IT leaders and PMO can make the first attempt. As I mentioned, everyone probably knows what the top few are. Put those on the list. Then list every project that is in-flight. Common sense would dictate that if a project is underway, it's more important than a project that hasn't started.

Rank Your List

Now we're going to employ a super-simple ranking tool. As you become more advanced, I recommend following a more sophisticated process called *weighted shortest job first* (WSJF), but let's start here. For each project, estimate the cost and the benefit. The benefit can be net positive cash flow, net income, or EBITDA. Whichever you choose, use the same metric for each project so you can compare disparate initiatives. Now divide the cost by the benefit to derive the relative value. Here's an example:

- Project A costs $100K and delivers $500K. Relative value = 5.
- Project B costs $100K and delivers $200K. Relative value = 2.
- Project C costs $300K and delivers $200K. Relative value = 0.66.

Use the relative value to initially rank the list. Distribute the list to your executive team and ask them to individually re-rank the projects from 1 through 25. Don't accept ties or "they're all number 1" as an answer. There can be only one number one. Also send your business objectives and business strategy documents. This will ensure that the executives consider alignment with business goals while they are ranking the projects.

WEIGHTED SHORTEST JOB FIRST (WSJF)

Weighted short job first (WSJF), popularized by the Scaled Agile Framework (SAFe) methodology, is an advanced concept for ranking and prioritizing disparate projects. Following this method, projects that provide the most value in the shortest time are prioritized the highest. In WSJF, the following items are given a relative rank using a Fibonacci sequence (1,2,3,5,8,13,20): business value, time criticality, and a combined score for risk reduction and opportunity enablement.

These three scores are added together to compute the cost of delay (CoD). Based on the scoring rules, the maximum CoD value for a project is 60, and the minimum is 3. Business owners are asked to score each of these items without knowledge of the effort and using a relative comparison to the other projects. For each of the parameters, the least valuable project receives a 1, and the most valuable receives a 20. The next step is to have the delivery team estimate the relative job size using the same sequence.

In the final step, the CoD is divided by the job size, giving the WSJF score. The projects should then be ranked descending by their WSJF score. If two projects have the same CoD, the project with the smallest job size is ranked the highest to maximize value creation.

Create a Standard Deviation Report

Once the results are back, create a standard deviation report. This will show you how far from the mean the leaders are for each project.

> **NOTE** I'm not asking you to do the math. STDEV is a formula for standard deviation in Excel.

As you can see from the example shown in Figure 30.1, everyone agreed that project A is the #1 project in the company. It's a clear winner, and there is no deviation. Project D needs more discussion: the CEO has it at #5, while the CFO has it at #2. When the deviation is zero across all of your projects, you have accomplished complete alignment.

	CEO	CFO	CIO	CPO	COO	CSO	Standard deviation
Project A	1	1	1	1	1	1	0.00
Project B	2	4	2	2	2	2	0.82
Project C	3	3	4	5	4	3	0.82
Project E	4	5	5	3	3	5	0.98
Project D	5	2	3	4	5	4	1.17

Figure 30.1: Example Project Ranking Worksheet

Communicate Priorities

It may take several rounds to get full alignment on your prioritized project list. Detailed estimates, in-depth ROI calculations, and heated discussions are part of the process. Once it's completed, shout the results from the mountain tops. Email the list to the officers in your company. Remove the numbers first, and then email the list to directors and managers across the organization. It's not a secret where their project is slotted on the list. Post the ranked list on the walls; and for our remote colleagues, post it on a virtual wall. Make it very clear: if it's not on the list, we aren't doing it. No more side projects. If an unlisted project gets started by a rogue executive, put that project near the top of the list, bump everyone else down, and communicate what happened.

Inside the IT Department, review the list in detail with everyone on the team.

Cumulative Total

Instead of starting with an annual budget and then seeing which projects will fit into that budget, list your projects on a spreadsheet in priority order, add the estimated cost of the project, and then add a cumulative total column. Create the list regardless of the budget. When the budget is established, simply draw a line at that point on the cumulative total. If you get more funding, move the line down, and the next project is included. If you get less funding, move the line up, and the lowest-ranked project will simply move into next year. Update the cost numbers monthly as actual results occur and more accurate estimates are created. This process will ensure that you never go over budget (in total) and that if you are tracking ahead on your budget, you will be prepared to take on the projects that were previously *below the line.*

Operationally Required Projects

Every company, regardless of industry, has a series of projects that are *must-do* and projects that are *should-do*. *Must-do* projects usually involve regulatory requirements. If you are required to send a new report to the federal government starting on January 1, creating that report becomes a *must-do* project. *Should-do* projects include things like upgrading an unsupported operating system and cyber-security initiatives. You really should do these projects; however, you don't have to. It becomes a risk management exercise.

In both cases, these are projects without a return on investment. I list these projects on a separate tab in the priority list and call them *operationally required* (OR). OR projects are reviewed and approved by the OR subcommittee. This committee consists of the CIO, the chief counsel, the controller, and the CFO. If you have an internal audit team, I recommend inviting them to the meeting, but their rules of impartiality mean that they shouldn't get a vote.

The OR subcommittee's job is to rank and prioritize these projects and indicate which ones are *must-do*. OR projects take precedence over all ROI projects. Label the first line of your priority list "operationally required" and bring the total approved forward. This becomes the starting amount in the cumulative total column. Every company needs to fund its *must-do* projects. If funds are tight, this may be all you do this year. Each *should-do* project needs to be evaluated based on the risk of not doing it. Going off support on a minor system may be worth the risk to the company. After funding the OR projects, the remaining investment funds will be dedicated to ROI projects.

Be Ready for Line Jumpers

People are smart, and if the formal process doesn't get their project on the list, they will deploy tactics to cut in line. Table 30.1 shows some of the common themes used to cut in line and my response to each of them.

Table 30.1: Responses to Line Jumpers

Tactic	Response
This is a departmental project, not an enterprise project.	We have one list for our entire company; every project that requires IT resources is included.
My project is not considered a capital investment, so it should be excluded.	We evaluate all projects based on their merits, not the accounting treatment.
This project is important to the CEO.	Good news, then; she's on the priority committee.
This project is small; it shouldn't go on the list.	We have a mechanism for handling small items within larger approved projects.
My project is a must-do project.	Bring it to the OR subcommittee.
My project has no ROI, but we should do it anyway.	Ask the CEO for an override—the CEO has the final say on the list regardless of the ROI.

If other executives have not bought into the process, they may approve a project regardless of the priority. If an unapproved project gets started, immediately put it as number one on the list, and let everyone know there is a new number one. Remember, all in-flight projects have a higher priority than every not-started project. If not, then why are you working on it? Talk to the executive and reaffirm the importance of the process. Let the other executives know that the line-jumper has delayed their projects. Hold an off-cycle priority meeting to discuss the impact. Over time, buy-in will improve, and line-jumpers will understand and support the ranked list.

Moving Forward

Once the list is created, it becomes easy to maintain. Hold a quarterly priority meeting and adjust the rank as necessary. Once a project is started, it can no longer be re-ranked. This causes thrashing, rework, and unwanted productivity killers. Compare the list to waiting in line for a roller coaster. You can bribe your way to the front of the line, or you can slip to the back. You can ask your friend to let you go ahead, or you can let your friends go ahead of you. You can even chicken out and ride the Ferris wheel, instead. However, once you sit in that seat and strap yourself in, there is no way off the ride until it is finished. There will be scary moments and moments of joy—when the ride is over, you'll feel elated and ready to conquer the next one.

Projects are like roller coasters, with ups and downs. With a ranked priority list and a solid WIP limit, we're ready to strap in and get our projects completed successfully. In the next chapter, we'll cover methods and processes to ensure that IT is doing everything it can to maximize value creation for your company.

31 Portfolio/ Program/Project Management

W hat's better, Agile or Waterfall? How about Program Evaluation and Review Technique (PERT), Rapid Application Development (RAD), PRojects IN Controlled Environments (PRINCE2), Extreme Programming (XP), or some of the other more obscure techniques? This shouldn't be an either/or question. All of these project management methodologies have value, and smart CIOs use elements from all of them to be successful. There's no sorting hat that declares you *Agile* or *Waterfall* before your project begins. Don't make project management a religion—*people* get projects done, and the tools they use are just that: tools. What tool do you prefer, a hammer or a screwdriver? It depends on the job (although hammers are way more fun).

It's important to carefully balance team-level autonomy with enterprise consistency. Teams should be permitted to create and follow their own processes depending on the type of work. A pure app dev team follows different methods than the team supporting SaaS software. Infrastructure teams have completely different needs than app dev teams. Grant these teams flexibility within the context of enterprise-level guardrails.

Regardless of your methodologies and specific needs, a number of concepts, tools, and approaches can help you manage your projects and your teams. Let's take a look.

Consistency Creates Speed

Standardize across your organization on terminology, forms, and meeting minutes. The exact form is less important than consistency across teams. Many of your internal customers will be involved in more than one IT project. It creates confusion when every team uses different lingo. *QA*, *dev*, *test*, and *sandbox* should mean the same thing from team to team. Do you prefer *bug* or *defect*? I don't care; just pick one.

Ranked Project List

At the enterprise (portfolio) level, you need a ranked project list. As discussed in depth in Chapter 30, this list provides clarity on what is most important. If the number one project requires virtual servers and your cloud engineer says they're too busy setting up the servers for project #25, something is awry.

A Unified Calendar

Imagine your company sells goods and services online. The web team is operating on two-week sprints that end every other Wednesday. This team is following advanced DevOps practices with an established Continuous Integration (CI) / Continuous Deployment (CD) pipeline. Your order management (OMS) team, also Agile (ish), operates on three-week (ish) sprints; if the release is not accepted, they adjust the deployment schedule until it is ready. Down the hall, the warehouse management team (WMS) is following a Waterfall model where they deploy code to production at the end of a major project, usually two or three times per year. When a new feature requires all three teams to make a change, you have a mess on your hands. Let's go back to culture for a moment. It's hard to imagine that these three teams feel like they're part of the same organization. The friction created by the different styles will create animosity and erode the culture you're trying to foster.

An easy first step is to unify on a single release calendar. In this example, I'd make the web team's calendar the department standard. From now on, everyone deploys to production every other Wednesday. If a team is not ready, they skip that cycle. At first, the OMS team may slip to a four-week sprint, and the WMS team still only deploys a few times a year. But at least they're all going to production on the same day, which is a good start. Once the calendar is unified, focus on automated testing for the OMS and WMS teams. Automated testing is the key to more frequent releases.

Big Room Planning

The best process I learned from SAFe is *big room planning*. This is a quarterly meeting that brings together all constituents across the organization to plan, prioritize, and review the work for the next quarter. Big room planning takes the prioritized project list down to the feature and story (use case scenario) level. It makes IT work visible. It's an extremely powerful opportunity to communicate everything IT does with your executive peers. We used blue painters' tape to draw a line on the wall. Everything below the blue line was out of scope for the quarter based on the team's capacity. Something unexpected happens when you openly and honestly tell your business partners what work you can't get to: they are now empowered to prioritize something else, come up with a manual process, or intervene to provide IT with more resources.

The Covid-19 pandemic has put a temporary halt on big room planning events. Clever people are devising virtual equivalents, but in-person meetings are still best. Post-pandemic, we will continue to have a more remote workforce. Big room planning is the ideal activity to bring cross-functional teams together four times per year.

Project Charter

Every project needs a charter. A charter is not just a legacy Waterfall tool. If the term *charter* sounds too heavy for your organization, use *terms of reference* or some other gentler-sounding name. Regardless of what you call it, the document needs to contain the who, what, why, when, where, how, and how much: the basics that explain the objective at the highest level and how to accomplish that objective. Keep this document concise. For some projects, it's important to include an *out-of-scope* section in the charter. Approved projects tend to get add-on work. The bus is leaving, and everyone wants a seat. I even advocate putting small items into your projects in Chapter 28, "What Should I Work on First?" While a few small things can be included, scope creep is the enemy of on-time and on-budget. Be clear about what's in and what's out in the beginning; this avoids misunderstandings later.

A Project Schedule Is Not a Project Plan —

I will happily argue that Microsoft Office is the best and most important business tool ever produced. On the flip side, Microsoft Project may be the worst thing that's happened to IT project management. Microsoft Project is a project scheduling tool, not a project management tool. The latest *Project Management Body of Knowledge* (PMBOK 7) includes 49 project management processes, and MS Project can help with fewer than five of them. In an Agile environment, there is no place at all for MS Project. I may be overly salty on this point, but I've seen too many projects go awry when the project manager became hyper-focused on creating a schedule at the expense of the other 48 processes. At the very least, Microsoft should change the name of this application to MS Project Scheduler.

Rant over. I have good news regarding tools: Microsoft 365 comes with a powerful new tool called Microsoft Tasks. This tool can be made visible from within Microsoft Teams, and it combines the Planner functionality with the To-Do functionality from Wunderlist. Whether your team follows Scrum, Kanban, or traditional methodologies, this embedded lightweight tool is a terrific way to organize and visualize tasks.

Kanban

Kanban is the Japanese word for a visual board or a sign. In project management, the word *Kanban* represents a process by which tasks are visually displayed on a board aligned into columns based on their status. Making work visible is a powerful tool for getting work done. A three-column Kanban board with *backlog, in-process*, and *completed* as the columns is an excellent way to get started with Kanban. When the team meets, team members move their assigned tasks from the *in-process* column to the *completed* column. Then they take a task they wish to work on next from the backlog and move it to *the in-process* column. The team member is selecting their next task; their supervisor is not assigning the task. This improves buy-in and, therefore, productivity. It's motivating to move tasks to *completed*, and it doesn't feel so good to have the work assigned to you sitting unfinished for very long. If your team meets in person, a large, on-the-wall Kanban board is preferred. If your team is virtual, then use a tool like Microsoft Tasks, or Microsoft Whiteboard using the included Kanban template, to create and display an online Kanban board.

Agile Mindset

Regardless of the specific tools and processes your team follows, CIOs and CEOs need to instill an Agile mindset in their organization. The Agile manifesto implores us to place a high value on human interactions and collaboration. By delivering working software more frequently, changes are less expensive and, therefore, well-tolerated in an Agile organization.

Entrepreneurs have learned that failure is a valuable learning tool, and they've embraced a fail-fast culture. Will large, risk-averse organizations be able to adopt these practices? Compare NASA's SLS program to SpaceX's starship program. After 10 years, NASA has spent over $18 billion without a single launch. By the time the rocket flies, the design will be obsolete. Meanwhile, SpaceX follows a *launch, explode, learn, adapt, and repeat* method. The iterative or Agile approach of SpaceX is creating a better, cheaper, more capable rocket than NASA's traditional approach. Agile is not all or nothing, as some of the Agile zealots would have you believe. Instill an Agile mindset in your organization, and iterate to more Agile practices over time.

Keep Teams Intact

In an attempt to improve output, I once added two people to a four-person team. My simple math concluded that this team would be 33% more productive. What happened? In the next sprint, their output decreased. What was going on? More people, less velocity? In 1965, Bruce Tuckman published the *forming–storming–norming–performing* model.[37] My scrum master explained that any change to a team, including adding resources, resets this model back to the start. In the long run, the team's velocity will increase, but in the short term, the change moves the team from *performing* to *forming*.

The worst thing you can do at the end of a successful project is disband the successful team. A team that delivers is a precious commodity. Keep the team intact, and flow work to it. In a pure Agile environment, we fund teams, not projects. The work they deliver is based on the feature backlog. It takes time and trust to get to acceptance for this practice in an annual budgeting, ROI corporate business model, but when you do, the output is impressive.

V Develop Key Business Proficiency for Maximum IT Efficiency

32

Love Your HR Department, Just Don't "Love" Your HR Department

You already know that I advocate embedding an HR business partner on your IT team. I didn't always feel this way. When I was a fledgling IT manager, I saw HR as an obstacle, a group of people who didn't get it. I'd ask questions like, "Why can't I just hire all my friends, give everyone on my team a large raise, and fire poor performers like they do on TV?" After all, who has time to give their employees honest feedback, performance reviews, and career coaching? We have "real" work to do.

My contentious relationship with HR didn't improve until I saw a better way modeled by my mentors. When Greg Rake took over the supply chain at Pier 1 Imports, he invited me to dinner with his leadership team. As I took my seat, I noticed something strange. Sitting among the supply chain team were HR business partners from across the country. The HR and supply chain leaders laughed, talked, and solved problems. This group of people worked together as a team. Greg was running a global organization with nearly 1,000 people, and he understood that people were the lifeblood of his organization. Running a supply chain wasn't just about ships, trucks, warehouses, and boxes. It was about leadership, culture, and performance management.

Around the same time, Pier 1 hired Sharon Leite, now CEO at The Vitamin Shoppe, as the EVP of store operations. Sharon partnered with HR at the highest levels from day one, embedding people practices into everything she did. Sharon introduced formal talent assessment and career development processes. Sharon spent countless hours reviewing and discussing the performance and potential of every store manager in the company.

Sharon brought field employees into the corporate office as part of their development. Sharon also sent corporate employees to work in the field, ensuring that they developed a 360 view of how our business operated. Making moves like this requires long-term thinking because, initially, productivity declines.

There was a point when one of these moves disrupted a project I was leading. A key resource was being rotated out to the field. When I tried to delay the transfer, Sharon was steadfast. She said the continued development of our people was more important than a single project. She supported the project while still moving forward with the change. How did it end up? The project was completed on time, and the employee became a vice president.

Partnering closely with HR was the unique advantage Greg and Sharon used to run successful organizations. It wasn't just the company that benefited: the care spent developing talent has been a career godsend for the people fortunate enough to work within their organizations.

When you partner with HR, it's crucial not only to work with the chief people officer (CPO) and your HR business partner; you should work directly with individual HR specialists as well.

Compensation

There's a general understanding that chief marketing officer (CMO) is one of the most challenging jobs in any company. The reason? Everyone believes they're a marketing expert. Colors, fonts, tone, medium: we all have strong opinions on how they could be better. Want to guess what single role is even more difficult and more thankless than marketing? It's the director of compensation (comp). Comp directors and managers have the dreaded *responsibility without authority.*

It is the responsibility of the compensation director to ensure the company is paying people according to its strategy, that titles and salaries are fair across the organization, and that incoming employees aren't blowing up the pay scale for the incumbents. They have to do this without direct authority over these decisions. The most important competency for a compensation director is *influence.*

If you're like I was, you may not even know who your compensation director is; or you override their recommendations. Stop doing this. A good comp director is like a good parent. Do your homework, brush your teeth, go to bed on time. None of these are fun, but they pay off in the long run. If you quit second-guessing your compensation experts, it will benefit you, your company, and your employees.

Employee Relations

Employee relations (ER) specialists are the people you deal with when something is amiss. Depending on your HR department's size and structure, this could be your HR business partner or a different specialist who focuses on this discipline.

We are human, and we all do stupid things. It could be an honest mistake made out of ignorance (employee didn't know the rules), a lapse in judgment (alcohol is often involved), or malicious behavior. Inappropriate behavior can also be rooted in mental illness, substance abuse, grief, or trauma.

After an incident occurs, it's the role of your ER partner to work through the cause, the impact, and the actions required. ER experts deal with large and small issues. From *Jessie's lunch stinks up the kitchen to Jessie embezzled $50,000 from the charity fund*, your ER specialist will help you navigate the rough waters. ER specialists must understand your company's policies and the applicable local, state, and federal laws. ER specialists work hand-in-hand with the legal department. When the CPO, the chief counsel, and an ER specialist show up at your office door, you're probably in for a rough day.

Many years ago, a young man came to me and offered to work for free. Let's call him Tom. We were implementing a popular finance system, and Tom wanted to become an expert on that system. We made a win-win deal: he would work 30 hours per week, unpaid, writing reports in this new system. If you read Malcolm Gladwell's *The Tipping Point*, you know it takes 10,000 hours to become an expert at something. Tom knew that he'd get much further working for free and developing a skill than sitting at home applying for jobs.

I treated Tom like any other contract employee. He was issued a contractor badge and a contractor cubicle and assigned to a manager. Nobody except Tom and I knew that his hourly bill rate was $0. I agreed that when Tom found a paying job, he could leave his *free* job without notice.

A few months went by, and someone on the team resigned. Tom was doing a fantastic job, and we decided to hire him as a full-time employee. This was the point when all hell broke loose. I show up in HR with an open job req and a person ready to fill it. The HR person looked at me sideways and asked, "Where did this guy come from?" I was so proud; I bragged, "He's been working here for three months—for free!"

The problem? There are laws against this kind of thing. You can't just have free employees. I argued and argued with my HR business partner. It harmed nobody. Tom asked for this arrangement. Tom benefitted from this arrangement. Finally, in my frustration, I appealed to the CPO. After hearing my plight, she looked at me and said, "Why are you complaining to me? I don't make the laws. Write your congressperson."

This was the big "aha" moment. HR is not the bad guy. HR is the protector. Whether hiring Tom for free was good for Tom or not, it was probably against the law. We asked Tom to submit a detailed timesheet for every hour worked, and we paid him based on the market rate. Tom felt bad, and at first he refused the money. He wanted to stand by our arrangement. We insisted, and Tom got a big check and a job. I had a painful budget miss that month, a slap on the wrist, and a whole lot of education. It all worked out fine; once HR helped me clean up my mistake.

In this example, I wasn't sneaky or malicious. I was ignorant of the rules and the consequences. What if Tom got hurt on the job? There was no contract in place to protect him or the company. The lesson here is not that you need to know every law and nuance. The lesson is to involve your HR business partner from the beginning. Any HR business partner would know that *hiring* Tom for free was a bad idea, and a 10-minute discussion would have prevented a lot of heartaches.

Learning and Development

Do you have a copy of your latest employee engagement survey? Let me guess: you have an opportunity to improve *learning and development*. IT professionals know they need to keep learning to be successful. A career in IT is a lifelong commitment to education. I fancied myself quite proficient in the legacy programming language, COBOL, back in 1990. Today, I'm not even qualified for an entry-level programming job.

Are you thinking about promoting a technical superstar to a supervisory role or having a business analyst run a project? I always advocate for internal promotions and lateral moves that provide career development opportunities for employees. To ensure that these moves are successful, you need to provide adequate training. The best way to get this done is to establish a partnership with the learning and development (L&D) experts in your HR department. They have the resources and knowledge you need. Even if it's technical training you're looking for, don't go off on your own. An L&D expert will help you craft a plan, find the right content, and make sure your development program aligns with the company's strategic direction for talent development.

Payroll and Benefits

Usually hidden behind a locked door, payroll and benefits experts are important business partners to get to know. The more you understand your benefits programs, the better conversations you can have with current and prospective employees. If an employee needs a leave of absence or special accommodation, work with your HR business partner and your benefits team to find the best solution. When you get the chance, be sure to thank these people. Executive compensation is complex, often requiring a disproportionate amount of time to calculate and process. Be cognizant that someone is putting in extra time and attention to ensure that you are being paid properly while they are making a fraction of what you make.

Organizational Design

I've dedicated several chapters of this book to organizational design. It's important to get this right; you need to work with an expert. The good news is that these experts probably already work at your company. Even if there's nobody in HR with an organizational design title, this is a competency for many HR professionals. Your CPO can point you to the best person. It may even be the CPO who will work directly with you on crafting your org.

Talent Acquisition

Regardless of the state of the economy, top talent is always scarce. Locating and attracting top talent to your company is the difference between having a mediocre team and an outstanding team. Make it your goal to improve your team when somebody leaves. Don't just backfill at the same experience level and compensation of the person who departed. Each new opening is an opportunity to balance the needs of the team. If you have low turnover, your teams are probably overweighted with highly experienced people. When an experienced employee departs, consider replacing them with an entry-level person. Having experience diversity on a team will create an opportunity for someone to coach, infuse new ideas, and lower the overall cost of the team.

Back when data centers were still a thing, we hired an intern on our server team. This kid was very excited when we asked him to rack a server: it was a big deal to him, and he approached the task with vim. Our veterans, who had racked hundreds of servers in their careers, considered this mindless grunt work.

When it's time to hire, don't just throw a job requisition over the fence to the talent acquisition team and then call every week asking where the candidates are. Before you post a job, determine what you need, update the job description, and work with compensation on the pay range. Then sit down with the recruiter and devise a plan to find the best candidates for the role.

Ask your talent acquisition department to source your contract staff. Talent is talent. Don't go it alone just because it's a contractor instead of an employee.

HR professionals have dedicated their careers to becoming experts on people. When you realize people are your key to success, you'll understand that HR is your most important business partner.

33

If I Wanted to Be a Lawyer, I Would Have Gone to Law School

Information technology contracts reside at the intersection of technology, accounting, and law. Before you sign a contract, it's wise to consult with experts from all three disciplines. My advice is to learn as many legal concepts as you can and teach your legal partners as much about technology as they're willing to absorb. The more you understand each other, the better you'll do when negotiating an agreement together.

For large, complex contracts, it may be beneficial to bring in outside experts. Some attorneys specialize in technology agreements. Work with these experts to create your own forms for mutual non-disclosure agreements, contract labor, consulting, and cloud software.

In a services contract, ensure that the work products have clearly designated ownership rights. When you hire software developers, does their company retain rights to the software you pay them to develop? They could, and I've been surprised by that clause in contracts. If the contract says they own the output and they've granted you a license, this means they can sell the software to other clients, potentially unbeknownst to you.

The rest of this chapter will explore licensing models and other legal concepts every CIO should understand to help you better work with legal and accounting teams.

Licensing Models

A primary construct in a software agreement is the licensing model. These range from simple and understandable business metrics to complex technical metrics. The amount of software your company is entitled to use is controlled by the agreed-upon measurement.

I'd like to commend Microsoft and Google for the licensing models they've adopted for their productivity tools, smartly packaged by need—you pay per user, per month. The current cost for the popular Microsoft 365 E3 license is $20 per month, about what you pay for Netflix premium. Microsoft allows you to adjust your license count up and down based on your user count. Importantly, these companies will verify that you already own an unassigned license before letting you use it. This is a benefit compared to licensing models where companies allow you to use whatever they want and then "true-up" later. But while the use-now, pay later model is sold as a benefit, it can get you in trouble quickly.

A somewhat controversial model, gain-share, is based on business outcomes. Let's use the example of an e-commerce website. You agree to pay the SaaS provider a percentage of total revenue. As the business grows, you'll pay a higher fee. This model makes the cost of the software a variable expense. When you do well, the provider makes more, making the *gain* shared between both parties. Advocates of this model argue that since the provider has a financial interest in your success, they will work harder to grow your sales. These companies have teams of people focused on your business's success. Through a quarterly business review process, they bring ideas and suggestions to the table. Detractors of gain-share believe you will overpay for the software as your business grows. I am a proponent of gain-share. Win-win models get everyone rowing in the right direction. Gain-share works when your company is growing, and it protects the company during a downturn. To avoid overpaying, negotiate a lower percentage of the share as volume increases.

In a data center environment, the software is often licensed based on the number and type of processor cores on the server. Avoid this model. You don't want hardware decisions to be dictated by a contract. In a virtualized and cloud world, this model falls apart quickly. How many cores are there in a virtual machine? It depends on whom you ask. There's a risk that your provider sees it differently than your server administrator. Technology evolves much faster than our contractual agreements.

The Cloud

Just when we were making progress on licensing models, along came the cloud, introducing an entirely new level of confusion into our world. You pay for creating an instance of a server or a service, for using the service, for the size and type of the storage, and anytime data moves.

Don't forget about paying for the software. For example, if you run Microsoft software on Amazon Web Services (AWS), you're going to have to pay Microsoft for the license and AWS for the compute. When cloud providers say you only pay for what you use, it's not entirely accurate. You pay for what you configure, how you configure it, and the actual consumption.

Indemnification

Indemnification is the legal term for who bears the risk and who pays when something goes wrong. Is the company selling the software, hardware, or service standing behind their product? Indemnification becomes especially important for intellectual property infringement claims. If you get sued for a patent violation, the verbiage in the agreement may or may not protect you. In the representation and warranty section of the contract, the seller should state that they have legal ownership and that they have the right to sell you the software.

Limitation of Liability

Sellers will try to limit their liability. Sometimes they will try to limit the liability to the purchase price of the software or one or two years of fees. If you agree to this, you will be on the hook for the remaining damages.

Breach/Litigation

When you are entering into an agreement, both sides are friendly and excited. Nobody thinks anything will go sour. It's the attorney's role to ensure that the contract protects the company in those situations. Contracts should stipulate how disputes will be handled. They document what constitutes a breach and the time to cure it. Contracts may require that disputes are handled through arbitration instead of the courts.

Force Majeure

Also called an *act of God*, force majeure is unforeseen circumstances—outside of the party's control—that prevent them from fulfilling a contract. Force majeure may exempt the party from liability. This clause usually needs to be specific—for example, a war. A rain shower in Seattle is not a force majeure event. Whether the Covid-19 pandemic will be a force majeure event will be argued for many years. Some contracts expressly stipulate pandemics; others do not.

Accounting Considerations

Be sure to have the contract reviewed by your CFO before you sign it. There are terms and conditions that affect financial reporting and journal entries. A warranty may have a different accounting treatment than prepaid support. Advanced payments or deferred payments affect cash, but most companies are accrual-based. When the salesperson offers *no payments until next year,* that does not mean it won't hit your budget until next year. Ensure that the payment terms, payment methods, and payment timing align with your corporate policies and capabilities.

Data Ownership and Preservation

Every year, ShopperTrak, a Johnson Controls company, puts out reports on store traffic (how many people visited stores). In January 2020, it reported on the prior holiday season: "Total in-store traffic in December was down 6.1% in the US and down 5% in Canada year-over-year."[38] How does ShopperTrak know this? It sells hardware and software to measure in-store traffic. Retailers rely on this data to manage their businesses. Because ShopperTrak stores this data in its cloud, the company can aggregate across all of its customers' data and produce insights like this. Does it have the right to do this? Absolutely, because that right is granted to the company by its customers in their contracts.

Is there any harm in this? It depends on the data and what Shopper-Trak is doing with it. As much as companies say that data is anonymized and aggregated, study after study has proven that it's easy to identify people even in supposedly anonymous data. "Researchers from two universities in Europe have published a method that can re-identify 99.98% of individuals in anonymized data sets with just 15 demographic attributes."[39] When you allow your data to be used and distributed, you potentially put your customers' information at risk. In addition, you're paying the provider to gain benefit from your data. As my legal friends might say, the *consideration* is backward.

Does your contract stipulate data ownership? Even if it unequivocally states that you are the sole and rightful owner of your data, you need to get it back when the agreement ends. A provider may charge a fee for data retrieval. This fee may be excessive and difficult to negotiate at the end of a relationship. If the data provides value to the provider, the provider won't simply delete it when your contract ends. If data deletion wasn't contemplated in the original contract, you might be out of luck. If the data has been anonymized, aggregated, and shared, there's no Undo button for that.

Cyber-Security

Pay special attention to cyber-security terms and conditions. What happens when the provider has a breach? Ensure that they are required to notify you of any cyber-incidents at their company involving your customers and your data.

Do you know where your data will be housed? If the provider plans to store your company's data outside of your home country, that can create sticky situations. Which country's laws and regulations govern the relationship? If you're using a service based or hosted in another country, make sure the contract is clear on these matters.

Unsavory Practices

It's common these days for software companies to provide their tools for free. The business model known as *freemium* allows free use of some features and a paid subscription model for others. Most times, tools are free for personal use only.

Do you, or people in your company, use freemium software to conduct business? If you said no, I'll bet you a coffee that you're wrong and that, unbeknownst to you, employees in your company are indeed using freemium tools. When your employees signed up, they checked the box committing your company, not themselves, to these terms. Here's a clause from a publicly available freemium contract:

> *If you signed up for a plan using your corporate email domain, your organization is [the] Customer.*

This is extremely important! If an individual signs up using their corporate email, the company is the customer, not the individual. Is this legal, committing an entire company based on a single employee's actions? Possibly not, depending on the person. If an executive accepted the end-user license agreement, it will be hard to argue they weren't authorized to commit the company to these terms.

If freemium software is an important business tool for your company, I recommend doing the following:

1. Pay for the enterprise version.
2. Negotiate more reasonable terms.
3. Educate your employees on the risks involved with using freemium tools.

We're not trying to be tyrants, but as leaders of a company, we're obligated to protect the company, its data, and its customers' data. For example, e-discovery requests and data hold capabilities that could be limited or non-existent in the free version.

End-User License Agreement (EULA)

Pronounced "yew-luh," this mechanism can get you in big trouble. It happened to me at a company that will go unmentioned. It was the middle of the night when critical software quit working. We were licensed and paid up on maintenance. Our technician called support, and they had a patch for this issue. The patch was sent over and installed by our tech. The system was back up and running, and the tech went back to sleep. Everything worked the way it was supposed to. Or so we thought.

A few months later, we were sued by the vendor for non-compliance. I was confused because we always complied with our software agreements. The lawsuit didn't match our contract terms. When we protested, we were told the contract we signed was no longer in effect. When installing the patch, our technician accepted a EULA that overrode the existing contract. Imagine spending months hashing out terms only to have it all overridden by a software patch in the middle of the night. Illegal? Possibly. Unsavory? Absolutely.

We settled the lawsuit. We deemed it more expensive to fight than to pay. What was the technician supposed to do? The patch doesn't install without accepting the EULA. Lawyers aren't going to get up at

3:00 a.m. and hash out new terms. To avoid this situation, insist that the original master agreement explicitly prohibits a EULA override. Another tip: do your research and avoid companies that make a profit by suing their customers.

Changing Terms on an Invoice

Like the EULA scheme, some vendors put different terms on their invoices. For example, the contract may say payment terms are *net 60,* and the invoice says *net 30.* Don't let this slip by. Request a new invoice, and refuse payment until the invoice is devoid of contradictory terms.

Virtualization

If your software agreements were written for physical servers and you intend to virtualize the application, be sure to check your contracts first. There's a good chance this affects the licensing model. Tools like VMware and Nutanix have revolutionized IT infrastructure, allowing us to build server farms that can support 15 or more virtual servers for every one physical server. This saves money, power, and administration. The good news turns sour when the software provider shows up and claims you owe them more money to run their application on your server farm.

Beware of similar challenges when migrating on-premises software to the cloud. Whether it's infrastructure-as-a-service (IaaS), platform-as-a-service (PaaS), or software-as-a-service (SaaS), make sure you address the legal and accounting concerns before undertaking a migration. These aren't just technical projects.

Hyperlinks

Don't sign a contract with hyperlinks. It's common for vendors to put their SLAs on a web page instead of directly in the contract. The vendor may agree to 99.999% uptime in a hyperlink and change it to 99.5% after signing the contract. If it's a large company, and they won't remove the hyperlinks, print every web page referred to in the contract and keep it in your records.

Relationships over Contracts

A respected attorney taught me that the relationship with the vendor is much more important than the contract. The best business relationships are governed by a contract that you'll never refer to. Build strong relationships with your vendors. When a problem occurs, call them before you call your attorney. If a dispute gets all the way to court, everyone loses.

Software Audits

Before you get audited, stipulate the rules around audits in your contracts. Use easy to measure business metrics wherever possible. Know and document your entitlements. Consider deploying a software asset management (SAM) tool for this purpose. Stay away from known bad guys. Educate your team to avoid these traps. And above all, do not use software you are not entitled to use. If you get a notice of audit, immediately call your chief counsel. Don't be overconfident that you'll be okay.

Your employees are just trying to do their job when they call support. Sometimes innocent questions during the support call can trigger a software audit. Make sure your entitlements are documented and understood by your teams. When talking to a salesperson or a support person, only provide the necessary information.

Other Involvement with the Legal Department

If you follow my advice and work closely with your legal team, you'll develop a good rapport with them. Just remember that they are not your lawyers; they are the company's lawyers. When the company's interests and your interests are aligned—as in a contract negotiation—this is not an issue. But when your needs conflict with the company's best interests, you may end up on the opposite side of the table from these same attorneys. If you find yourself negotiating with the company, consider getting your own attorney.

You will also work with the legal department on employee relations issues. Once again, they are representing the company. If your interests are aligned, they are the best partner you can have in these situations.

CIOs are wise to invest time learning everything they can regarding legal matters. If HR is your most important business partner, then the legal department is a close second. In the next chapter, we explore negotiations. You wouldn't go outside in the winter without putting on a jacket—don't show up at a negotiation without first consulting with your legal partners.

34 Let's Make a Deal

Whether you're buying a hat, a new car, or millions of dollars of cloud services, IT leaders need to be competent negotiators. To complete a successful negotiation, you need:

- Time
- Information
- Objectivity
- Choice

Are you working against a real or an artificial deadline? A real deadline could be a hard date on the calendar, like a government mandate, or it could be a business date, like the end of the quarter. The deadline could be artificially imposed by the salesperson, or it could be internally imposed based on hitting a project date. Don't box yourself into a corner with artificial deadlines. Time is a tremendous asset in a negotiation, and if you give up this advantage, there better be a worthwhile reason.

I was recently in a negotiation for a tool that was a low priority for my company. Since it wasn't a priority, we didn't pay much attention to the negotiation. When we didn't respond, the providers continued to lower the cost. Like the person who can't stand awkward silence, they kept responding to our inaction with lower and lower prices. Had we been in a hurry, we would have paid more. We weren't using advanced negotiation tactics; we were doing nothing—a successful and low-effort approach.

Don't fall for artificial deadlines imposed by salespeople. In 20-plus years of doing this, I've never seen a price go up after an arbitrary deadline had passed. Is it quarter end? There's a new quarter in 90 days. Is there special year-end pricing? It had better be ridiculously special, or I'll talk to you in January. When you have a legitimate deadline, start early. Time is an asset, and the clock is always ticking.

Information is king in any negotiation. If you know the seller's bottom number, then you're at an advantage. In negotiation theory, the overlap of the buyer's and seller's acceptable ranges is known as the *zone of possible agreement* (ZOPA). You're not a good negotiator if you stick to a position outside of the ZOPA and never get a deal done. A winning negotiator strikes a deal at the lowest end of the seller's range. To gather information, ask open-ended questions. Salespeople are extroverts—they love to talk. If you're stuck, scheduling an executive-level meeting with the seller is an excellent tactic. They have more information and more authority to lower the price.

If you're emotionally attached to the solution, the company, or the salesperson, you need to assign the negotiation to another person. Once your reptilian brain takes over, you're in a bad place to negotiate. When you "gotta have it," you're going to overpay for it. There are independent, professional negotiators who work on commission. If you're too close to a deal, hire an outsider to negotiate on your behalf.

The most important asset in a negotiation is choice. Understand your options. If you're negotiating with an incumbent provider, options may be more limited, but work hard to give yourself leverage in every negotiation. Use non-financial incentives to gain an edge. A press release, speaking at a conference, and case studies are all valuable to technology sellers. Don't give away these things for free.

Once the deal is signed, you're going to have to cough up some money. Be sure you have the accounting skills to manage all of your expenses, big and small. In the next chapter, we'll review the basic accounting knowledge every CIO should have.

35 Accounting, My Worst Subject

In the fall of 1997, I was working as a manager of applications at Express, Inc., which was a division of Limited Brands. Our director (my boss) and our CIO (his boss) both resigned in rapid succession. Three of the managers—Gary, Bob, and I—were summoned to the CFO's office. In 1997, Express wasn't the open-door culture that companies cultivate these days. The CFO's office was a scary place that I had never visited before.

The CFO informed us that we were now directors and should divvy up the IT Department accordingly. I spoke first and said I'd take the planning, merchandizing, and replenishment systems. Bob jumped in and claimed purchasing and distribution, leaving Gary with point-of-sale and the general ledger. The three of us were happy with the arrangement, since we were essentially already doing these jobs. Gary then added, "I have a degree in accounting. I can manage the IT expenses."

I was relieved. The prior director and the CIO had managed the expenses. I barely scored a C in my only two accounting classes, and I was already working long hours. The last thing I wanted to do was some double-entry accounting.

A few weeks passed, and I asked the CFO if I could send a few team members to a training class. His reply was, "Is it in the budget?" Looking back, that's a common CFO question that I should have been prepared to answer. I said, "I have no clue; I'll go ask Gary." Gary told me, "Sorry, there is no money for training—they can't go." Not long after, I was trying to promote a team member, and again I found myself asking Gary if we had the funds.

What was going on? Was Gary somehow my boss? I quickly learned that in business, *whoever is in charge of the money, is in charge.* To this day, I don't know if Gary was brilliant or just helping, but either way, by being an expert in accounting, he granted himself authority over the department.

Chargebacks

Are you looking for a fun night out on the town? Take a few CIOs to a bar, buy them a few drinks, and then ask what they think about chargebacks. To charge back or not is a hotly debated topic with strong opinions on both sides. A *chargeback* is an allocation of IT costs back to the business unit owners. Some CIOs swear by this practice, running a net-zero IT Department where every dollar spent is allocated to a respective business unit. Others, like me, believe this is a horrible idea.

Chargebacks (allocations) may be required for accounting. Chargebacks are also an important concept when you are running a shared-service organization for a multi-division company. The service is shared, and so is the cost. The chargeback could be inter-company, intra-company, or charged to an external entity. I'm sure each Marriott hotel franchise kicks in a few bucks for IT to the mother ship.

When you allocate the budget to another department, you lose control. What if your chief revenue officer believes their software will run less expensively in the Microsoft cloud than it does in the Amazon cloud? Are you now switching cloud providers? We love our business partners, but we don't want them selecting our technology. If they're paying for it, they will get a say. Remember the lesson from Gary McGee: *whoever is in charge of the money, is in charge.*

Another problem with chargebacks is confusing reporting. Take the example of a $20 million monthly budget with $2 million charged back to operations. After the chargeback, the net budget is $18 million. Through sound expense management, you save $400,000 and only charge back $1.6 million. Your results come in at $18.4 million since you charged back less than was planned. What? You saved $400,000, and it shows you over budget by $400,000? On the flip side, if you overspent on that budget line, you'd look like a frugal leader with a firm command of the budget. To avoid frustration and confusion, manage expenses before the allocations occur.

Showbacks

The alternative to the chargeback is the showback. Keep the budget in IT, but report on where the money is being spent. Showbacks are the best of both worlds, involving your business partners in IT costs while maintaining control. A pie chart showing IT operating expenses is an insightful and powerful tool.

Remedial Accounting Starts Here

For the rest of this chapter, I will review the must-know accounting terms and concepts. If you're Gary or otherwise an accounting expert, please skip to the next chapter.

General Ledger

The general ledger (GL) consists of units and accounts. For example, IT would be a unit (or department), and travel_expense would be the account. If the GL is set up cleanly, every department would have a travel_expense account. It's a simple hierarchy that your IT brain will understand. Ask your controller to give you a copy of the *chart of accounts* for your company.

Accruals

Because we use accrual-based accounting, income and expenses are recorded when they occur, not when the money changes hands. If a consultant works in May and you pay them in June, that's a May expense. If you prepay for a year of software support, your accounting team will spread these charges evenly over the next 12 months. When vendors offer *no payments for six months*, be careful: you may be unknowingly entering your company into a financing deal. Don't sign it without agreement from the controller and the treasurer.

Balance Sheet

The *balance sheet* is the schedule—accountants call reports schedules; be cool like them, and do the same—that shows what you own (assets) versus what you owe (liabilities). If you have a truck, it's an asset. If you took out a loan to pay for the truck, that's a liability. These principles apply to IT when we purchase capital equipment, including servers and network switches. They become assets on the balance sheet.

Income Statement

The *income statement* shows how much you made or lost in the period: what came in versus what went out. Revenue – (expenses, interest, depreciation, amortization, taxes) = net income. In large corporations, the income statement is accrual-based. You book the expense when it happens, not when it is paid.

Statement of Cash Flows

The *statement of cash flows* shows how much actual money the company has on hand. If you borrow $50 million and put it in the bank, the net on your balance sheet doesn't change. You add $50 million to the left side (asset) and $50 million to the right side (liability). What changes is the cash on hand. Having enough cash to operate your business is known as *liquidity*. You may have a healthy balance sheet, but if it's all tied up in fixed assets, you risk not having enough cash to pay your employees and your suppliers.

Together, the *balance sheet*, the *income statement*, and the *statement of cash flows* provide a full picture of a company's financial health. These three schedules are sometimes referred to as the holy trinity of accounting schedules.

Capital Expenses (CapEx) vs. Operating Expenses (OpEx)

If you buy something tangible, and that item will be around for at least two years (fiscal periods, for our fancy friends), then it's an asset. An asset could be a building, a truck, a server, a network switch, or a piece of software. The last one is tricky. Is software tangible? It depends; if the expense is to purchase software that's installed on a server or a laptop, it's considered an asset, CapEx. If it's to purchase use of cloud software, (e.g., Microsoft Office 365 for employees to use Teams or email), then the expense is OpEx.

If something's not an asset, then it's an operating expense. Electricity is OpEx; office supplies are OpEx; patching servers is OpEx; attending a training class is OpEx. Think of it this way: nouns are CapEx, and verbs are OpEx. *The server was rebooted by Sally.* The server is CapEx, the act of rebooting is OpEx.

> **NOTE** The cloud has increased the confusion. Here's an explanation that may help. Although the accounting for implementation costs has been standardized, the accounting for the hosting fees will not be consistent. In a cloud arrangement that includes a software license, the hosting fees attributable to the software license must be capitalized as an intangible asset with a corresponding liability to the extent the fees are paid over time. In contrast, if a hosting arrangement does not include a software license, the hosting fees are expensed as incurred.[40]

Capitalized Internal Labor

CIOs need to be experts on the rules surrounding capitalizing internal labor. In short, if your employees' work is involved in creating or improving an asset, that time spent is treated as CapEx, not OpEx. In the case *the server was configured by Kendall,* The noun (*server*) and the verb (*configured*) are both considered capital expenditures. *Configuring* adds value to the server; rebooting does not. These rules are complex, and they change frequently. To learn more, read up on ASC-350-40. Drop that term in front of your controller, and you will impress. Because of this accounting rule, your employees must track the hours they spend on capital projects.

Depreciation

Let's talk about our truck again. When we buy a truck, it becomes an asset. If the truck costs $50,000, and we're going to get 10 years of use from it, we don't book the truck's entire cost in the year we bought it. We spread the cost evenly over the life of the truck. This is called *depreciation.* It's important to note that the depreciation of our truck is calculated differently for tax purposes. *We're going to ignore that in this book.* We will subtract $5,000 from our income statement to account for the truck for the next 10 years. This makes sense because we're getting value from the truck over its entire life.

Write-Off

When my mother was still alive, she used to think that when I went on a business trip or out to a business dinner, it was free. She'd say, "It's a write-off, Andrew." My mother didn't go to business school or any other college. Still, somewhere along the way, she learned that companies deduct their expenses before they calculate income, and therefore, these items reduce the tax burden on a company.

When I talk about write-offs, I'm not referring to business expenses; I'm referring to taking an asset out of service before it is fully depreciated. If we gave our truck a 10-year life, and it dies after 7 years, we need to record all of the remaining depreciation at that time. The truck has been *written off*. If a long-running IT project fails, all of the costs hit the bottom line when the project is canceled. If there is no asset, there is no depreciation. Fear of the write-off is one reason failing projects are not canceled. These projects instead get prolonged, throwing good money after bad. If my mother were alive today, she'd probably school us all on the sunk-cost fallacy.

EBITDA

EBITDA, pronounced "ee-bit-dah," stands for earnings before interest, taxes, depreciation, and amortization. It's a mechanism that excludes these items to show how well management is running the company. If the tax rate declines because of an act of Congress, earnings will go up, even though management did nothing different. Depreciation is also excluded from EBITDA to encourage capital investment. We need that truck to grow our business.

Return on Investment (ROI)

ROI is a schedule created before a project is approved to ensure a good investment. The mix of Opex and CapEx in an IT project makes these schedules challenging to follow. An alternative is to use a cash-based ROI model. Build a spreadsheet with 36 months across the top, and then record the monthly revenue and expenses over the project's life. Besides the total return, this model will show your maximum cash outlay required for the project, and it will show you when you break even.

Lookback ROI

Once your project is completed, create an ROI schedule with the actual results. Compare it back to your projections. Learning from each project will improve your future projections and inform you about which future projects to undertake.

To succeed as an IT leader, you need to make accounting your favorite subject. Get to know your CFO and your controller. Hold monthly budget meetings with your IT management team and their corresponding finance partners. Understand where every dollar is spent and how it's being recorded.

To build an Amazing IT team, you need to be a business expert. A firm accounting foundation will expand your business knowledge. In the next chapter, we'll explore more ideas for becoming a business expert.

Learn Your Business, Inside and Out

When was the last time you unloaded a truck, scrubbed a toilet, or answered the customer service hotline? Immersing yourself in the day-to-day tasks is the surest way to become educated about what goes on in your business. Did you just deploy tablets to your workforce? Get out to the field, where you'll use it yourself. That case you bought to protect the tablet becomes mighty heavy after eight hours. And the internet speed in remote locations is slower than the broadband speeds you enjoy back at HQ or at home.

At The Vitamin Shoppe, we have a formal program for our corporate employees to work in the stores. When I worked for Brookdale Senior Living, all of the executives spent a week in a senior community, working with the staff and interacting with the residents. These moments with the seniors were very moving, increasing my resolve to do my best to provide them with a high quality of life. Regardless of what industry you're in, interact with your external customers.

The pace is much quicker in a retail environment than in a retirement home. If your IT help desk answers a call in three minutes and resolves the problem in five minutes, you're probably feeling pretty good about those metrics. Now view that interaction from the other side of the phone. You're working at a cash register, and the system locks up while you're ringing out a customer. You call the help desk and go through a confusing phone tree. You are now on hold as the seconds slowly tick by. The customer, ready to go, begins to fidget and look at their watch. Soon another customer joins the line, and the queue is two-deep. As you're following the troubleshooting steps, the customer at the front of the line drops their items in disgust and walks out the door. More customers join the line, and now the queue is four-deep. Finally the register works again, but you have an unresolved transaction to clear, and there is a negative buzz in the store because all the customers are frustrated. What feels like a win for the help desk is a nightmare in the store.

Another way to become an expert in your business is to read everything that your business publishes. If you work at a public company, the financial reports are filled with valuable information. If there is something you don't understand, ask your CFO. Even better, jot down all your questions and take the CFO to lunch to review them.

Learn about the history of the company. Read old documents, and get long-time employees talking. Knowing the past will help you become a true expert on your company.

Ask to attend meetings across the organization. Involve yourself in every aspect of the company: sales, marketing, operations, and manufacturing. If you don't attend board meetings, you need to get in there, even as a fly on the wall. Ask your CEO to include you as part of your career development. When you're invited, be on time, be polite, and keep your mouth shut.

In Part VI, "Straighten Up and Fly Right," we explore the professional behaviors that all aspiring leaders need to adopt.

VI Straighten Up and Fly Right

37 What You Should Have Learned in Kindergarten

I didn't go to kindergarten. I have no idea why, and my parents aren't around to explain. Fortunately, my parents taught me to say *please* and *thank you*, to share my toys, and to wait my turn. As you achieve business success, it's easy to believe basic manners don't apply to you. Like the celebrity who proclaims, "Do you know who I am?" business leaders can become accustomed to preferential treatment. If we're not careful, this can turn us into jerks. Here's a simple test:

1. Do you frequently lose your temper at the office?
2. Do you go to the front of the buffet line during corporate functions?
3. Do you ask your employees to work weekends and then neglect to thank them on Monday morning?
4. Do you have a nicer laptop than you issue to your subordinates?
5. Are you dismissive of your team?
6. Do you interrupt?
7. Do you consider your peers your competition?
8. Does someone else get you coffee in the morning?

To paraphrase Jeff Foxworthy, if you answered yes to any of these questions, you might be a jerk. According to Stanford professor Robert Sutton,[41] being a jerk is often glamorized in media. Who doesn't admire the accomplishments of Steve Jobs? His poor behavior is overlooked because we love our iPhones.

The problem for aspiring jerks is that it doesn't work. Acting this way will not turn you into Steve Jobs. Sutton explains, "Hundreds of experiments show that encounters with rude, insulting, and demeaning people undermine others' performance, including their decision-making skills, productivity, creativity, and willingness to work harder and help coworkers."[41]

If being a jerk isn't productive, why are people still doing it? As the kids like to say, "These people have issues." If you fall into this camp, I encourage you to work on your behavior through stress management, exercise, and therapy. Leaders need to keep perspective. Early in my career at The Limited (now L Brands), people loved to rant and rave over the smallest of mistakes. One day, while being berated, I looked at my boss and said, "It's just girl clothes." Sure, my algorithm incorrectly sent 100 sweaters to the wrong store, and yes, that sucks, but in the context of all the problems in the world, this one wasn't worth turning red with anger.

There's no reason you can't be a polite, considerate, assertive leader. Being nice is not being a pushover.

> **NOTE** When I was young, the worst thing you could be called was *nice*—as in, "That Andy Laudato, he's a nice guy." *Nice* was a euphemism for unattractive or otherwise unappealing to potential dating partners. Nice felt like the opposite of strong and assertive. I was so traumatized by being called nice that I asked my daughter to engrave on my tombstone, "Here lies Andrew Laudato. He was not a nice man."

When Bill Clinton got in trouble for having a relationship with an intern, a pundit on television said that Clinton would survive impeachment because he was liked. The pundit compared Clinton to Nixon. Nobody liked Nixon, so when he screwed up, he was out. Hopefully none of us are doing things as egregious as these two, or as other more current political figures in the headlines these days, but when we do make mistakes, will the people around us fight for us to stay or revel in our demise?

One of the ironies of life is that the more money you make, the fewer things you have to buy. As a COO, I can get a salesperson to take me out to breakfast, lunch, and dinner every day of the week. I could eat caviar for breakfast, FleurBurgers[42] for lunch, and fresh lobster for dinner, and their companies would gladly pay for it. I often wonder where these people were back in my college days when I didn't have much money for lunch. Just remember why they're buying you Fleur-Burgers. It's not your good looks, personality, or engaging conversation. A salesperson's job is to convince you to shell out your company's cash for their products and services. As you move up the career ladder, stay grounded, and don't let your success go to your head.

The skills you learned in kindergarten will go a long way toward making you a better leader, reducing your stress, and even prolonging your life. In the next chapter, we'll go beyond the basics related to keeping yourself grounded to exploring what it really means to behave professionally.

38 Professionalism Isn't Just Wearing a Suit

Although she deprived me of kindergarten, my mother went out of her way to teach me *please* and *thank you*. She made me write thank-you notes and say *hello* and *good-bye* to my friend's parents when I visited their homes. But one thing I missed out on growing up was eating in restaurants. As Italians, we believed eating "out" meant inferior food at a higher cost. What's the point in that?

This lack of restaurant experience led to two embarrassing moments for me: the first incident occurred at senior prom, and the second while I was working at Jo-Ann Stores. My prom dinner with a date and two other couples was going okay until there was a problem with the check. Being a cool customer, I called the waitress over and said, "There's a problem with this check. We were charged for *gratuity,* and none of us ordered the *gratuity*." Trying not to laugh, she explained that gratuity means *tip,* and the restaurant always added that in for parties of six or more. It was a new vocabulary word for me. In my defense, we never had *gratuity* at home. Isn't that French?

If that's not embarrassing enough, my next opportunity to make a fool of myself came when I was the director of applications for Jo-Ann Stores in 1998. We were at dinner with a large group, and I was seated next to Betty Rosskamm. Mrs. Rosskamm is Jo-Ann royalty. She's the daughter of the co-founders and the mother of then-CEO Alan Rosskamm. She also worked at the company. It was a *prix fixe* menu, and when it was my turn to order, the waitress asked me if I wanted "chicken, pasta, or beef, well-done." I was savvy enough to know you don't order well-done beef in a restaurant, so I said, "I'll take the beef, medium." The waitress repeated back to me, "Beef-well-done?" I was lost. Sparing me from my misery, Mrs. Rosskamm said, "She's saying *Beef Wellington*." Ahh, Beef Wellington! Another food I had never heard of. I had the chicken.

Knowing that a gratuity is a tip and that Beef Wellington is a tenderloin wrapped with prosciutto and puff pastry is a good start. Other tips for being professional at dinner are learning which forks to use, waiting for others to be served before eating, being kind to the waitstaff, and chewing with your mouth closed. It's wise to eat a snack before a business dinner, so you don't devour a loaf of bread and all the appetizers. If you're on somebody else's tab, don't order the three-pound Maine lobster and the Château Lafite-Rothschild. In addition to table manners, here are some important traits a leader needs to exemplify,

Complain the Right Way

It's okay to complain about work if you complain to the right people. If you complain to your subordinates, you demean them and yourself. Being a victim is not a strong leadership quality. When there's a problem, tell someone who can do something about it: your boss.

Don't Allow Gossip

Rumors are always worse than the truth. If your organization is rife with gossip, it's probably because there isn't enough communication flowing from leadership throughout the rest of the organization.

Make Your Word Gold

The military uses a type of missile called *fire-and-forget*. Such a missile is programmed to find the target on its own. Once it is launched, it will find its way. The pilot can move on to the next task without worrying about the missile. This needs to be you. When you get an assignment from your boss, get it done—every time. If it's taking more than a week, proactively provide status. If it turns out to be a bad idea, let your boss know. Don't just drop the ball. We've all had subordinates we needed to follow up on. This adds stress and workload to the leader. Create a good tracking system, and follow through every single time.

Keep a Secret

Loose lips sink ships and companies. Confidentiality is a must for executives. I have an age-old trick I'm going to share with you on how to keep a secret. Ready? Here it comes:

Don't tell anybody.

Got it? The moment you tell your trusted friend, your parent, or your spouse, you did not keep the secret. If you told one person and the secret gets out, how do you know it wasn't your fault? If you fail to keep secrets, you'll be left out of the loop and, therefore, left out of the room. Your goal of earning a seat at the table will be thwarted.

Don't Yell, Curse, or Pound the Table

If every other word out of your mouth is an f-bomb, you've rendered the value of that word down to nothing. Sparsely using expletives can be an effective technique. Be the leader who seldom curses, and when you need to get someone's attention, it will be there for you. Side note: if you run into a wall or stub your toe, let loose. Science has proven that cursing can lessen pain.[43]

A more effective approach than losing your temper is to express your disappointment. If someone screams at me, I'll become angry and defensive. However, if my boss tells me that I let her down, that hurts me to the core.

Assume Everything Will Get Out

Imagine if everything you said and wrote was read aloud on the news each evening. Your family and friends would tune in as the reporter read your email rantings. Would you be proud or embarrassed? Would it be suitable for children, or TV-MA? Before you hit Send on that next email, close your eyes and use this filter to decide if you want to send it. This is not just an exercise; corporate emails often become public. Adopt the mantra *no negative emails*. If you need to have a tough conversation, do it in person.

Remove Stress from Your Boss

Mark Cuban said the most valuable employees are the ones who reduce stress.[44] "If you are a stress reducer, you're going to do well. If you're a drama creator, you're not going to do well," Cuban said. "Anybody who reduces my stress becomes invaluable to me. I never want to get rid of them."

Just a Little Bit Better

The best way to be professional without being a pretentious, out-of-touch snob is to take a *just a little bit better* approach. If the norm at your company is to wear jeans and a polo shirt, then be sure you wear high-quality jeans and a pressed polo. Don't show up in a formal suit—dress *just a little bit better* than the norm. You'll fit in and demonstrate professionalism. If your boss is in the office from 8:30 a.m. to 5:30 p.m., consider working from 8:25 a.m. to 5:35 p.m. For an extra 10 minutes a day, in your boss's mind, you are always at the office. If the company norm is to show up at meetings right on time, arrive two or three minutes earlier. Being *just a little bit better* will make a huge impression.

Professionalism is important, because like it or not, everyone is watching. In the next chapter, we'll discuss why professionalism is a full-time job.

39 What You Do Matters— You're Always on the Clock

It took me a while to get comfortable with my stalkers. Fort Worth, Texas, is not that small a town, but my staff always seemed to know my whereabouts. "I saw you were shopping at Central Market yesterday; how was that steak?" "Is your daughter sick? She missed school today." And this was before social media. Now, stalkers don't even need to leave home to know what you're up to. When you become an executive, you're always on the clock.

People love to talk. A simple tip is that the number of people who work for you is equal to the number of people who talk about you. Get comfortable with it. If you don't like people talking about you, management is not your thing. Don't be a jerk, and they'll mostly say good things. Learn to develop thick skin. Remember, complaining about the boss over cocktails is a favorite after-work pastime.

Your out-of-work behaviors become part of your at-work reputation. If you're a jerk to a waiter, odds are, it will get back to the office. I'm not suggesting that you have to change your behavior outside of the office. Just be aware that the higher up the ladder you climb, the more the line between the *work you* and *personal you* blurs. If it's your goal to be professional, you need to make it a full-time job.

As an IT leader, you will often deal with aggressive salespeople; we will discuss how to approach this in the next two chapters.

40 Vendors and *Frendors*

On an average day, I get 20 or 30 solicitations from vendors of IT software, hardware, and services. This is partially my fault because I put myself out there on LinkedIn, through public speaking, and now a book. It's easy pickings to say, "I read your book; will you please give me 10 minutes of your time?" Over the years, I've developed methods to respond to cold calls that I believe are fast, effective, and fair to the vendor. I once had an older relative tell me, "Be nice to salespeople; they're just trying to make a living." On the other hand, I've got a job to do, and I'm awfully busy. I can't spend my day in a series of 30-minute meetings with strangers from LinkedIn.

When I ask other CIOs how they handle cold calls, the most common response is to ignore them. The problem with ignoring salespeople is that they will move on to pester your peers, boss, and team. The problem with responding is that you can get sucked down a rabbit hole. Above all else, do not lead salespeople on. Kicking the can to next quarter can go on indefinitely. If you say, "Call me back in a few months," that gets entered in a CRM tool, and they will call you back in precisely 90 days.

If a note is sent to *Dear [Firstname]* and contains misspellings or other basic errors, I promptly delete it without a response. If a note begins *Dear Thomas*, I delete it because my name is Andrew, so it obviously wasn't meant for me. This happens all the time. If some effort was put into the note and it's still not something I'm interested in, I say so and ask to be removed from the mailing list. If I do think there is value for someone else in my company, I reply with this carefully crafted response:

> As a courtesy to you, I've sent your message to the appropriate people via blind copy. As this is not my area, you will receive no further

replies from me. Please don't be surprised or offended if you don't hear back from us. We get hundreds of cold-call solicitations every single day.

I have this response saved as an email signature in Outlook so I can respond in less than 15 seconds. Fair and efficient. More than once, this has led to a conversation because the person I blind copied was interested: a win-win. I'm clearly not making a referral, and I will not respond further to this person. If people persist, I have them blocked, removing their ability to email me or anyone in our company. If they're extremely rude, I'll block their entire company.

I don't recommend answering your office phone or calling back sales-people. I don't answer my office phone, and I've removed the number from my business card and my email signature. I can't remember the last time I got an important message on my office line. My CEO, my peers, and my team can easily reach me through other methods. Strangers can reach me on LinkedIn and via my work email address. I do not conduct business on my personal cell, my personal email, or Facebook.

If you have a long and successful run with a partner, you may end up developing a close relationship with them. I call these people *frendors*. Frendors are like friends, with the exception that they're still trying to sell you something. It's important to be cognizant of this aspect of the relationship because letting your guard down could become detrimental to your business relationship. We'll discuss vendor relationships in the next chapter.

41 A Word to the Vendors

Vendors! You've got to do better. Here is a solicitation I received on LinkedIn, selling business process outsourcing:

This will also help you to save a lot of money—like
you don't have
to hire full-time
employees or add extra space to your office, chairs,
electricity, and whatnot.

The poor grammar aside, I'm going to "save money on chairs?" Chairs and whatnot? Somebody is paying this person money to send a note like this to a COO of a billion-dollar company. And this is not a one-off example.

At least once per day, I get an email asking me *who does what* at my company. For example, "Can you tell me who is responsible for cyber-security at your company?" What's wrong, is Google broken? I suspect the person asking already knows the answer, but they're trying to swindle me. If I say that Shelly Sandstone is our CISO, the unscrupulous salesperson will write to Shelly and say, "Andrew gave me your name." Not a lie, but a sneaky trick.

My friend and mentor, Vicki Cantrell, had a successful career as a CIO and COO at luxury retail brands. Vicki then held an executive role at the largest retail association, the National Retail Federation (NRF). Following that stint, Vicki worked for a software vendor. Having seen the industry from all angles, Vicki had a big "aha" moment. The people who drive the retail industry—retailers, vendors, analysts, and reporters—all have vastly different goals and perspectives. Having been on all sides of the table, Vicki was shocked to find out how little each group knew about the others. General mistrust and lack of empathy led to skepticism and adversarial relationships. Instead of forming productive partnerships, retailers and retail vendors remain wary of one another. Vicki noted that the relationship between digital leaders and their vendor partners was much healthier. Why? According to Cantrell, "It's because they built the digital industry together during the dot-com boom." Vicki is so passionate about improving relationships that she, along with Phil Leahy, co-founded Vendors in Partnership, an organization dedicated to "those that are willing to make changes that are meaningful in creating a better partnership with retailers, increasing the success of all."[45] Vicki understands that we're all going to do better when we all work better together.

If you want to get your foot in the door with a CIO, gimmicks, jokes, and multiple-choice options aren't going to work. Making threats and bashing your competitors is a losing proposition, as is talking to the CEO's executive assistant and then telling me the "office of the CEO" told you to call me. Really? An office did that? Listing everything wrong with my website is another fast path to the electronic trash bin. Sending me half of a gift is the worst. "Here's a remote-control car; meet with me for the controller." No, thank you. If you send me cakes and cookies, I'll share them with the team. That's not a bad way to start. Just don't be the person who sent me a cake with their photo painted on top in frosting.

The foolproof way to get a meeting is to have another CxO contact me on your behalf. If your product or service is good, you should have several executives willing to brag about it. I'm just asking for one. I relish every opportunity to speak with another business executive. If an executive reaches out to me, of course I'm going to take the call. When I hear from your customer about success, I'm a believer. Drop the gimmicks, and earn good references. That's the key to growing your business.

42

Be a Cool Customer

I'm constantly impressed by executives who stay cool and collected. Their offices are clean, and they always seem to have time when you need it. My boss, Sharon Leite, is one of the hardest-working CEOs in the business. In addition to running The Vitamin Shoppe, Sharon sits on multiple boards, speaks at conferences, and is involved in charity work. The other day, I sent Sharon a note on Microsoft Teams: "Do you have a minute?" Her response: "Of course!" Of course? For all I know, Denise, her executive assistant, had to move two meetings and stop a plane from taking off to make room for my conversation. But Sharon wouldn't let me know that. She didn't ask what I wanted to talk about. It could have been a major emergency, or I could have been asking her for a cookie recipe. Whatever I needed to talk about, she made the time. If Sharon can find the time for her people, then so can I, and so can you.

Why might you be *too busy*? Let's diagnose it:

- You don't trust your team.
- Your team is not up to the task.
- You've bitten off more than you can chew.
- You're a bad delegator.

Delegation is a critical executive skill. If you're frazzled, you'll appear to be over your head, and your job will be in jeopardy. One simple way to delegate is to hold a staff meeting and go through your to-do list one line at a time. Ask your team members to volunteer for any items they feel they can tackle. Keep track of the assignments in Microsoft Planner or any other basic task tool, and review progress each week. By delegating, you're giving your team members valuable experience. By delegating, you're providing new opportunities. By delegating, you'll be available the next time a team member says, "Do you have a minute?"

During meetings, especially one-on-ones, be fully present. If you find yourself multi-tasking, stop. Now that we're all on video, keep your camera on. Not just so others can see you—so you can see yourself. Keeping your camera on should help keep you honest. It is harder to multitask when others are watching. Multitasking is ineffective and impolite.

Before we were an item, my fiancée and I worked together on the project described in Chapter 20, "The Power of Experts." She gave me valuable advice: "Slow your roll." I thought she was describing my driving leadership style, but she corrected me: "No, literally, slow your roll." She observed me at the office, rushing hurriedly from meeting to meeting. I would put my head down, lean forward, and move as quickly as I could without breaking into a run. Her advice was to slow down and act like an executive, not an overly caffeinated crazy man sprinting from meeting to meeting.

In football, players perform elaborate celebrations when they score a touchdown. Some spike the ball, others jump into the stands, and most have a signature dance of some kind. Not Barry Sanders. He would simply hand the ball to the referee. As legendary football coach Vince Lombardy said, "Act like you've been there before." Scoring 109 touchdowns in his NFL career, running back Barry Sanders was a cool customer.

When you get invited to the board room, be a cool customer and act like you've been there before.

In the next chapter, we'll discuss the importance of health and wellness for executives.

43 Get Your Butt in Shape

An exercise chapter in a business book? Like it or not, to successfully lead an Amazing IT Team, your physical, emotional, and cognitive health need to be at their optimum levels. Many of us don't become executives until we're in our 40s, 50s, or older. As we age, our bodies require more care. Let's cover four pillars of health and wellness: sleep, weight management, nutrition, and exercise.

> **NOTE** Disclaimer: I'm not an expert, and this chapter is not medical advice. These are my opinions based on my personal experience and observations. They are not the opinions of my company, my friends, or my doctor. I carefully use plenty of weasel words, including *could*, *may*, and *might*.

Sleep

Are you aware of the basic mechanism of exercise physiology? When you run, bike, or lift weights, you are injuring your muscles, tendons, and ligaments. Then you go to sleep, and your body builds them back stronger. Adaptation is a core function of the human body. What's your body using to accomplish this task? The nutrients you feed it during the day, especially protein. So hit the weights, consume protein, and go to sleep. While you are sleeping, your construction crew rebuilds your body. What if you aren't getting enough sleep? The workout was wasted. You'll remain injured and not repaired, leading to stress. What if you only eat low-nutrient foods? The same thing: the workout caused more harm than good. You will not get any benefit from exercise if you aren't getting sufficient sleep and nutrition. If you are planning to add exercise to your routine, first figure out how and when you're going to sleep.

If you have trouble sleeping, exercise may be the cure for that too. More sleep is conducive to better weight management. Positive health changes all work synergistically.

Weight Management

If you need to lose weight, just exercising more is probably not the answer. To lose weight, you need to eat better food. When you eat better food, you're going to eat less food automatically. Why? Because your body is smart. When it has what it needs, it won't ask for more. If you eat french fries until you're sick, you still haven't given your body what it needs—1,000 calories worth of fries later, you're still hungry. If you had a healthy salad, you'd be satiated on a fraction of the calories. Weight management is complicated, and every one of us is different. Regardless of your situation, you can't go wrong eating more nutritious food.

Nutrition

The Covid-19 pandemic has highlighted the importance of a strong immune system. "Research has shown that supplementing with certain vitamins, minerals, herbs, and other substances can improve immune response and potentially protect against illness."[46] To boost their immune systems, many consumers are turning to vitamin C, vitamin D, zinc, and elderberry.

If you go to an older doctor, you might have heard that you can get all of your nutrients from the foods you eat. This may have been truer when your doctor went to medical school, but it's becoming less so every day. "A 2004 study evaluated Department of Agriculture data for 43 garden crops from 1950 to 1999. The researchers found statistically reliable declines for six nutrients—protein, calcium, potassium, iron, and vitamins B2 and C."[47] Others disagree and say the issue is that we don't eat enough fruits and vegetables. Regardless of why, being undernourished may undermine your weight management efforts and render your exercise less effective.

If you're considering supplementation, look to nature first and then supplement from there. If you don't eat enough fruits and vegetables, a good quality multi-vitamin might help. If you eat wild-caught, fatty fish three or more times per week, then you're probably fine on omega-3 fatty acids. If not, consider a fish oil supplement. If you get out in the sun, vitamin D is free; if not, a vitamin D supplement is an option. I recommend this formula: get what you can from nature, and then supplement where needed.

Exercise

If I could figure out how to put exercise in a pill, I'd be richer than Jeff Bezos. The list of benefits from exercise is long and impressive. The best exercise is the one that you'll do. If you incorporate exercise into your life in a way that also brings enjoyment and stress relief, you've found something magical. A long walk, a bike ride, a group class, strength training—if one or more of these gives you joy, it will be easy to add the routine to or keep it in your life.

If the pandemic turned you into a part-time or full-time work-from-home employee, consider investing the saved commute time in an exercise routine. I strongly recommend a morning workout. You may believe you're not a morning person, but most successful executives are. You're much more likely to have an unplanned meeting, assignment, or happy hour at 6:00 p.m. than you are at 6:00 a.m. A regimented morning routine will do wonders for your day. Remember the importance of sleep for your health? To be a morning person, you're going to need to get to sleep earlier.

Put your health first. Being a CIO is like driving a car 100 miles an hour for 12 hours a day. It's only going to work if it's well maintained and there's fuel in the tank. Put on your business hat—set health goals, and attack them with the same vigor you use to go after EBITDA. Annual checkups with a doctor are mandatory. Consider these your body's performance review, and strive to *exceed expectations*.

VII Final Tips and Advice

When Something Goes Wrong

This chapter is not about the small or medium-sized issues that CIOs deal with every day. It's about those big, hairy, lump-in-the-throat incidents you hope to never have in an entire career: when something goes wrong with your systems, and it leads to a serious problem.

Depending on your industry and the incident, we could be talking about a security breach, loss of revenue, SEC concerns, significant customer inconvenience (e.g., a power outage), or even loss of life. The idea of a robot killing a human is no longer science fiction. It's already happened. In his *Forbes* article "Who Is Responsible When Robots Kill?"[48] Jack Garson answers, "It's not the robots." Regardless of your title, if you're the head of IT at your company, you need to own the problem. If the fire is still raging, don't worry about blame, remorse, or what you should have done differently. There'll be plenty of time for lamenting when the fire is out.

When something goes wrong, it's best to have a step-by-step approach to handle it.

Step 1: Leap into Action

Activate your crisis response team. Hopefully, you've prepared in advance, and you have a script for dealing with major incidents. If not, remember, no lamenting; you'll need to do this on the fly. When assembling a makeshift crisis response team, the CEO, CFO, CISO, CPO, and general counsel (GC) are all obvious choices. Don't forget about your public relations (PR) person. Even if it's internal only, an expert writer is a key team member. If you're not sure whether the incident is big enough to bother these executives, err on the side of telling them. A fire truck at a false alarm is better than no firefighters at an inferno.

Don't worry about being the CIO who cried wolf. At the same time, don't overdo the communication until you've fully assessed the problem. Keep the crisis response team small. An email to the ALL_EMPLOYEES distribution list is not appropriate in the early stages.

Step 2: Assess Things

Assess the situation. How bad is it? Who else do you need to include on the response team? What are your next steps? If the incident is over, you need to work on the clean-up activities. If it's still underway, divide the group so the CIO and the IT team can focus on putting out the fire while the rest of the response team focuses on communication and the next steps.

Step 3: Plan Your Response

Formulate a plan. Once you have a reasonable handle on the incident, discuss and review all of the alternatives. Let everybody speak. While this is most likely urgent, don't go so fast that you make additional mistakes that compound the problem. Remember when an Air Asiana plane crashed in San Francisco, and firefighters ran over and killed a survivor?[49] The unlucky woman survived a plane crash only to be killed moments later by her "rescuers."

Step 4: Communicate

Be sure to communicate the right information to the right parties. The response team will determine the who, what, and where of communication. As a CIO, you probably don't know best. Lean on your GC and PR experts. This is what they do.

Step 5: Monitor the Situation

Continually reassess the situation. Ongoing incidents are fluid; the team needs to constantly assess and reassess the situation. If the conditions have changed, go back to step 3 and formulate an updated plan.

Step 6: Learn from It

When the incident is over, take time to learn from it. The best results that can come from a bad thing are the knowledge and tools to prevent it from happening again.

When we're under stress, our bad qualities tend to emerge. Keep your cool and your integrity during the crisis. Be present and available, and learn from the experience.

In the next chapter, we'll discuss the importance of proactively preparing for an external review of the IT department.

45 When Others Come Knocking

If it hasn't happened already, the time will come when an outsider is tasked with evaluating your IT department. This evaluation could be part of due diligence for a possible merger or acquisition, mandated by the board, or a for-profit company that talked your CFO into an IT department review with the promise of huge savings and faster project delivery.

Like an incident response plan, the more you prepare in advance, the easier it will go. The prep work for an external evaluation is not wasted time. The information you're going to be asked to provide is information you should already have available. Start working on it now. If you need a list, there are plenty on the internet. One challenge with due diligence is that you will probably be asked to provide all the information without involving your team. Preparing in advance will help you know where to look when the request comes in. If you can't provide the data on your own, get permission to *read someone in* to the process. Acquisitions and IPOs require the highest level of confidentiality. If you tell half your team what's going on, there will be a leak.

At the least, you'll be asked to provide your IT strategy, organizational charts, past and future OpEx and CapEx budgets, current project list, and ROI for each project. Sound familiar? I've addressed each of these items in this book. Putting together an IT strategy is the most important task you can do to prepare for an external evaluation. The evaluators will also request an inventory of all your hardware and software and copies of all your current contracts. They'll want details of your cyber-security program, a list of prior incidents, and a copy of your cyber-insurance policy.

The evaluators may ask for something you don't have and don't believe in. For example, *provide a copy of your resource model for the next 12 months*. If you're running an Agile shop, resource modeling looks different than it does in a Waterfall environment. My recommendation for requested items that you don't have is to write a memo explaining why. If they ask for a *level 1 data flow diagram*, and you don't have it, don't rush to slap something together. Write a memo explaining the situation, and provide the memo as your response to that request. Only create new documentation when your own management asks for it. You don't work for the auditors. At least, not yet [joke].

In summary, be careful without being defensive. Their job is to find problems in your department. They are going to judge you based on their criteria, not the criteria you've established with your leadership team. Think of due diligence the same way you think of the home inspector when you're buying a house. They're being paid to protect the buyer, not the homeowner. They are looking for risks and weaknesses on behalf of the buyer. If the company has underspent on technology, this will come out in due diligence and potentially affect the transaction price. Ironically, if, in their opinion, your company is overspending on IT, it will be seen as an advantage.

In the next chapter, we'll discuss outsourcing the IT department, and why I believe this idea should be kicked to the curb.

46 What's Wrong with Outsourcing?

I spent years being politically correct on this topic, but no longer. The idea of completely outsourcing your IT Department is one of the worst business decisions a company can make. I've yet to hear a CEO brag about how getting rid of technology was a successful business decision. This is the digital age, and companies need to embrace technology, not ship it off to save a few bucks.

Let's walk through the basic economics of full-scale IT outsourcing. As CIOs, we provide our services to our company at cost. An outsource provider must build a profit margin into its model. It also has sales and marketing expenses. Ross Perot used to take CEOs for helicopter rides when he was pitching outsourcing. Helicopters and aviation fuel do not come cheaply. In addition to these markups, the outsourcing model requires ongoing, nonproductive overhead, including account reps and liaisons back to the company. To make the model work while still saving the promised 10–25%, the people doing the work must be paid much, much less than insourced talent.

In an outsourcing arrangement, requirements need to be more detailed, which is another hidden cost of the model. I had an SAP business analyst tell me that his requirements are so detailed, they could compile. For my nontechnical readers, that means the analyst is doing the work of the offshore developers in addition to his own work. Language, cultural, and time zone differences create ambiguity and re-work.

If you have a repetitive task, it's logical to get it done as cheaply as possible. However, once you outsource a task, you lose the ability to eliminate or automate the task. It's out of sight, out of mind. With robotic process automation (RPA) and artificial intelligence (AI), a computer can now perform tasks that until recently required a human.

This is less expensive and more reliable than even the cheapest labor pool you can find in any country. For example, you can pay someone in Bulgaria $6 per hour[50] to handle your paper invoices, or you can move to electronic data interchange (EDI) and process them for pennies.

I contend that hiring fewer, better people is the best way to staff an IT Department. When you aim for the lowest possible hourly rate, you end up with the opposite: quantity over quality. As your team gets bigger, your per-person productivity decreases. The reasons behind this are explained beautifully by Alina Vrabie:[51]

> *If you're putting together a project team, then you're most likely considering ideal team size. Do you go with a large team, hence more brainpower potential, or a small team? At first sight, more people might seem to result in better or faster outcomes. But both research and experience show that small teams are in fact much more efficient than large teams.*

Full-scale outsourcing saddles you with a team that has not bought into your company's mission and culture. Why not? Because they don't work for your company.

One smart career move for CIOs is to spearhead bringing IT back in-house. Legendary CIO Randy Mott successfully insourced IT at General Motors. Mott explains, "We went to a fully insourced model from what was previously a 90 percent outsourced IT workforce. We were on the far end of the spectrum in terms of outsourcing, and we have swung to the other side of the pendulum."[52] Mott said his IT Department now provides ten times more value at a lower cost. Funny that it sounds like the argument the company probably made when it outsourced IT in the first place.

In the next chapter, we'll discuss switching jobs; whether you're promoted internally, or taking the leap to go elsewhere.

47 Switching Jobs

Average CIO tenure has remained steady at around five years, worse than every other C-suite role.[53] CIO longevity was even shorter back in the dot-com boom-and-bust period, and there's anecdotal evidence that the Covid-19 pandemic has accelerated CIO turnover once again. The race to digital is on—and CIOs who aren't driving the digital train will be run over by it.

If you're a sitting CIO, this is your reality: you need to keep your suit pressed and your résumé updated. If you're on the path to becoming a CIO, this is good news—opportunities are out there. Recruiters will often say, "The client will consider a strong number two." Up-and-comers are younger, more in-tune with digital, and more diverse. These attributes are very attractive to companies right now. "As has been the case for several years, application development provides the most common route up for today's CIO, with 43% of CIOs coming up through this function."[54]

If you're an up-and-comer looking to become a CIO, CTO, CDO, or whichever three-letter abbreviation for IT leader is in vogue right now, times have never been better. Remember, what got you here won't get you there. Focus on developing leadership skills, and be brave enough to let your hands-on tech skills atrophy.

If you've been in the business for decades, you need to stay modern and relevant. The ill-fitting suit and cream-colored résumé you used for your old job aren't sufficient for the next one. While I love to reminisce about big iron, those mainframe days are long gone. You need to be digitally fluent and business savvy. Don't use buzzwords, especially not ancient ones. If you utter *I-series* or *NonStop Himalaya* in your interview, it's game over.

Should I Stay, or Should I Go?

You may be considering leaving your current job for a better opportunity. Here are some reasons to leave:

- IT is not valued at your company.
- You don't see eye-to-eye with your CEO (also called *philosophical differences*).
- Unethical behavior is tolerated at your company (e.g., racism, sexism).
- You're about to get fired.

Here are a few good reasons to stay:

- You lead a high-performing team.
- You have a seat at the table.
- You believe in your company's mission.
- You have opportunities to take on more responsibilities (e.g., COO).

Make the Move

If you decide to switch jobs, take the advice of my grandmother and thousands of other grandmothers: "Do not leave your paying job until you have a new one." Even if the money isn't an issue, it's much harder to find a role when you're unemployed. I had an executive recruiter say, "The client is only considering sitting CIOs." Harsh? Absolutely. But such is life.

Remember, the skills you need to do the job, and the skills you need to get the job, are different. Buy a new suit, polish your résumé, lay off the cookies, and network your butt off. If you haven't interviewed for a while, hire a professional interview coach, and practice.

One of the first questions you should ask the recruiter is, "Why is the job open?" Understanding what happened with the prior CIO is critical. Ask this question of each person you interview with. If the prior CIO was fired for moving the company to the cloud, and you're an outspoken cloud advocate, this might not be the right role for you. If the prior CIO left on their own without a new role, that's a red flag. It's a big deal to get a CIO role, and it can be tempting to ignore warning signs. You need to be confident that it's the right fit for you and your career.

On-Board Yourself

Once you land a new job, the first 100 days are critical. Everyone gets a honeymoon period. Here's my 10-step plan for newly minted CIOs:

1. Put out any fires.
2. Perform a mini due diligence.
3. Assess the team.
4. Throw away your personal pre-existing preferences.
5. Immerse yourself in the business.
6. Find a quick win.
7. Make a plan.
8. Get buy-in.
9. Eliminate your enemies.
10. Go! Don't dilly-dally. Take action.

You read that right. I just said to *eliminate your enemies*. Yes, this is absolutely essential. If this were ancient Sparta, I'd tell you to identify any enemies and put a spear through their hearts. In a twenty-first-century business setting, this is more easily accomplished with a short conversation and a severance check. I'm not talking about poor performers. Poor performers should be given a chance to excel in your new organization. You may find that they were in the wrong role or lost their mojo due to bad culture. By *enemies*, I mean individuals on your team who overtly undermine your leadership. This happens for numerous reasons: misogyny, jealousy, or a general philosophical difference about how things should be run. You're the boss, and you have to take the reins. If you end up with an enemy, they need to be dealt with swiftly.

Another situation you might face is the prior CIO is staying at the company in a different capacity. Prior CIOs who don't leave create unique challenges. Your first order of business is to identify faults in their organization. This is awkward and uncomfortable. If the CIO is staying on in a reduced capacity, as an advisor, in another department, or as your boss, spend a considerable amount of time with this person before you accept the role, and be sure that you agree on the best ways to run IT.

If you were promoted internally, you need to do a few extra things:

- Overtly get out of the weeds. Over-correct in this area to make it clear that you've taken a step up.
- Make a visible change. Move offices, dress a little nicer, stop attending operational meetings.
- Replace your prior position. If you're still doing your old VP of applications or VP of infrastructure job, you're a CIO in name only.
- Up-level your relationships. Your peer group has changed.

At 8:00 a.m. Monday, on the first day of your new job, you own everything. Don't be like the politicians who constantly complain about the problems they inherited. It's your shop now. Every system, process, and person belongs to you. Make sure you change your pronouns to match your new situation. Say *we* when talking about your new company, and say *they* when talking about your old company. Try to avoid talking about your old company as much as possible; it makes you a bore. When I say, "Back at Pier 1, we were the greatest," I roll my eyes at myself. It's off-putting. Besides, Pier 1 went bankrupt; we couldn't have been that amazing. One simple fix is to use the phrase "In my past life" or simply "In the past." Your experience is important. A slight wording change can make a big difference in how you are perceived.

Martha Heller, the founder and CEO of Heller Search Associates, has a wealth of content on her website, `https://www.hellersearch.com`, for CIOs in new roles. Additionally, Heller has written two terrific books for IT leaders: *The CIO Paradox* and *Be the Business*.

In the next chapter, we'll discuss why it's important to keep your high-level technology knowledge up-to-date.

Technology Matters

I was in a job interview the first time I blurted out the phrase "Being a CIO has nothing to do with technology—it's 100% about people." The interviewer's eyes lit up. This was different—a technologist saying his job was a people's job. She ate it up. I was thrilled; I had finally unlocked the key to landing any CIO job. The next time I had an interview, I simply gave my canned answers to the canned questions and waited for my chance to utter the magic phrase. *Being a CIO is a people job!* Bam! It worked every time. The reason? Too many of us lead with technology and fail to relate to business problems. CIOs need to use technology to solve business problems, not the other way around. Aligning IT and the business was a top topic at conferences in the 1990s, and it's still a top topic 30 years later. The problem with my magic statement is that it's not entirely true. If being a CIO is only a *people job,* why don't we see HR professionals flocking to CIO roles?

CIOs need to understand technology, just like CIOs need to understand business concepts, accounting principles, negotiation, project management, and—of course—people management. A career in technology is a life-long commitment to learning. You get it; you're near the end of a business book. Books are a low-cost, self-paced, easy way to learn. Books are the tools humans have used to pass down knowledge for millennia. Books are just as relevant today as they were 2,000 years ago. Another low-cost, easy way to learn is through online education. Not only are these online platforms cost-effective, but they also allow all of us to become instructors. I teach a project management course on Udemy.

CIOs who invest time learning the basics of web development, cybersecurity, and networking will be better IT leaders than those who don't bother. No, we shouldn't be learning so deeply that we'd qualify to be hands-on experts: that's not the best use of our time in our positions. But learning the basics keeps us current, and it helps us be empathetic leaders. The US Navy requires that an aircraft carrier commanding officer be a naval aviator (Navy term for a pilot). The Navy believes that first-hand flying experience is vital to running a floating airport in a war zone. In a similar but much safer fashion, CIOs are expected to make the final decision on technical matters. Be sure to learn enough to make the best possible decision for your company.

If you truly want to be an expert in something, take the next step, and teach it. Teaching is the highest form of learning. To explain a concept to someone who doesn't understand it, you have to have mastery of the subject.

Being a CIO is a people job, but technology matters, too.

49 Conclusion

At the top of the Laudato Hierarchy of IT Needs pyramid is *innovation*. Innovation should be the goal of all IT leaders—since innovation is required for companies to thrive and sometimes even to survive. To foster innovation, CIOs must first *keep the lights on (KTLO)*, run a *lean and efficient* IT Department, and *create value* for their company. Like any pyramid, this one needs to be built from the bottom up. Each layer provides the building blocks for the next higher level. Although it may be tempting to start at the top, jumping into innovation without completing the previous steps will not be successful.

KTLO starts with people, not technology. The first step is to understand and document service-level objectives, risk tolerance, and uptime requirements. You can't succeed until you know what success is. Once these details are agreed on, the CIO should devise a plan to accomplish them. No IT Department is perfect; minimizing the impact and learning from failures is essential for KTLO.

Once systems are reliable, CIOs need to turn their attention to cost management. As I like to say, "Get it right, then get it cheap." Running a lean and efficient organization increases the CIO's credibility, and it frees up funds for investing.

With reliable and affordable systems, CIOs can now move up to creating value. Value creation comes in the form of cost reduction, risk reduction, and increased revenue. New capabilities are identified and delivered through IT projects. Well-run projects maximize value and protect the hard-earned reliability and affordability that are in place.

None of this is easy. To get to the top of the pyramid, CIOs must establish the proper organizational structure and populate it with talented employees. These employees need to be aligned and motivated, and they must fully understand both the mission and their role in delivering the mission.

When these things are accomplished, an Amazing IT Team will emerge: a team that is happy, motivated, and continuously innovating.

Notes

1. Robert Austin (Harvard Business Review Press, 2016), The Adventures of an IT Leader, Updated ed.
2. G. Bock, K. Carpenter, and J. E. Davis, "Management's Newest Star: Meet the Chief Information Officer" (*Business Week*, 1986, October 3), No. 2968, 160–166.
3. Nicholas G. Carr, "IT Doesn't Matter" (*Harvard Business Review*, 2003), https://hbr.org/2003/05/it-doesnt-matter.
4. H.R.3763 - 107th Congress (2001-2002): Sarbanes-Oxley Act of 2002 | Congress.gov | Library of Congress. https://www.congress.gov/bill/107th-congress/house-bill/3763/text.
5. A. H. Maslow, *Motivation and Personality* (Harper & Brothers publisher, 1954), 411 pages, ISBN 978-0-06-041987-5.
6. A. Laudato, "Why CIOs Need to Pour Concrete," (Heller Search Associates, May 27, 2020), https://www.hellersearch.com/blog/why-cios-need-to-pour-concrete.
7. Brent is a character in *The Phoenix Project: A Novel About IT, DevOps, and Helping Your Business Win* by Gene Kim, Kevin Behr, and George Spafford (IT Revolution Press, 2013), https://www.goodreads.com/book/show/17255186-the-phoenix-project.
8. Security Roundtable (Palo Alto Networks), https://www.security-roundtable.org.
9. *Mad Men* refers to the fictional AMC TV series that portrays the advertising industry in the 1960s.
10. The Spanning Tree Protocol (STP) is a network protocol that ensures a loop-free topology for any bridged Ethernet local area network.
11. Michael M. Lombardo, Robert W. Eichinger, "The Career Architect Development Planner" (1st ed.) (Lominger, 1996), Minneapolis. p. iv. ISBN 0-9655712-1-1.
12. Popularized in the 1980s by management consultants Tom Peters and Robert Waterman. Tom Peters and Robert H. Waterman "In Search of Excellence" (1982, 2004), (360 pages), p.289, web: BooksG-FOC-289.

13. The concept of lean was pioneered by Toyota, the Japanese automotive giant, as a means to reduce waste in manufacturing. The concept was adapted to suit various industries, including IT. It aims to remove all things unnecessary, all the fat, from software engineering. Its principles resonate largely with those of Agile development.

14. Taiichi Ohno (Productivity Press, 1988). Toyota production system: beyond large-scale production. Portland, OR. ISBN 0-915299-14-3.

15. Elena L. Botelho, Kim R. Powell, and Tahl Raz, "The CEO Next Door: The 4 Behaviors that Transform Ordinary People into World-Class Leaders" (March 6, 2018), ISBN 1101906502.

16. Bradford D. Smart Ph.D. Topgrading, 3rd Edition: The Proven Hiring and Promoting Method That Turbocharges Company Performance (Aug 16, 2012), ISBN1591845262.

17. https://www.inc.com/marcel-schwantes/warren-buffett-says-if-you-hire-somebody-without-this-trait-you-really-want-them-to-be-dumb-lazy.html.

18. David Brock and Paulette Gerkovich, "Why Diverse Teams Outperform Homogeneous Teams" (*Your Brain at Work*, 2021), https://neuroleadership.com/your-brain-at-work/why-diverse-teams-outperform-homogeneous-teams.

19. MAX451 is now Doyenne360 (http://doyenne360.com).

20. Joseph Sirosh "How Azure ML Partners are Innovating for their Customers" (Microsoft Machine Learning Blog, July 14, 2014), https://docs.microsoft.com/en-us/archive/blogs/machinelearning/how-azure-ml-partners-are-innovating-for-their-customers.

21. "Finding a Better Connection with Customers Through Cloud Machine Learning (1-Business)", YouTube video, 1:58, "Microsoft Customer Stories," September 15, 2016, https://youtu.be/dJMZVaBWBH4.

22. "Finding a Better Connection with Customers Through Cloud Machine Learning (2-Technical)", YouTube video, 2:08, "Microsoft Customer Stories," September 15, 2016, https://youtu.be/CdYvPgXc5ic.

23. Doug Henschen "Microsoft Azure Machine Learning: Pier 1 Digs In" (InformationWeek, July 14, 2014), https://www.informationweek.com/big-data-analytics/microsoft-azure-machine-learning-pier-1-digs-in.

24. Brandpost, Microsoft, "The Cloud's Game-Changer Is Competitive Advantage" (CIO, June 5, 2015), https://www.cio.com/article/247108/the-cloud-s-game-changer-is-competitive-advantage.html.

25. Thor Olavsrud "12 Microsoft Power BI success stories" (CIO, August 16, 2017), https://www.cio.com/article/230488/12-microsoft-power-bi-success-stories.html.

26. "Pier 1 Imports: Finding a Better Connection with Customers" (Chain Store Age, August 1, 2017), https://chainstoreage.com/exclusive-content/pier-1-case-study.

27. Alicia Esposito "Pier 1 Imports Redesigns Business Intelligence With Microsoft" (Retail TouchPoints, September 25, 2014), https://www.retailtouchpoints.com/features/retail-success-stories/pier-1-imports-redesigns-business-intelligence-with-microsoft.

28. Security Roundtable (Palo Alto Networks), https://www.security-roundtable.org.

29. This quote is most commonly attributed to Kenneth Blanchard.

30. "It's the Economy, Stupid," (Harvard Political Review, Oct 17, 2012). https://harvardpolitics.com/its-the-economy-stupid/.

31. https://www.cdta.org/sites/default/files/awards/beyond_the_12-factor_app_pivotal.pdf.

32. Gartner (press release, 2020), https://www.gartner.com/en/news-room/press-releases/2020-10-07-gartner-says-worldwide-data-center-infrastructure-spending-to-grow-6-percent-in-2021.

33. National Institute of Standards and Technology (NIST): https://www.nist.gov/cybersecurity; HiTrust Alliance: https://hitrustalliance.net/product-tool/hitrust-csf/; Center for Internet Security CIS): https://www.cisecurity.org/; ISO 27001: https://www.iso.org/isoiec-27001-information-security.html; Control Objectives for Information Technologies (COBIT): https://www.isaca.org/resources/cobit.

34. Amazon Web Services, EC2 Auto Scaling, https://docs.aws.amazon.com/autoscaling/ec2/userguide/what-is-amazon-ec2-auto-scaling.html.

35. Little's Law - D. Simchi-Levi, M. A. Trick "Introduction to "Little's Law as Viewed on Its 50th Anniversary" (Operations Research, 2013), 59 (3): 535. doi:10.1287/opre.1110.0941.

36. https://kanbantool.com/kanban-guide/kanban-history.

37. Bruce W. Tuckman "Developmental sequence in small groups" (Psychological Bulletin, 1965), 63, 384–399.

38. Marianne Wilson, "ShopperTrak, December store traffic falls" (*Chain Store Age*, 2020), https://chainstoreage.com/shoppertrak-december-store-traffic-falls.

39. Rae Hodge, "It's not that hard to unmask real people in anonymous data" (CNET, 2019), https://www.cnet.com/tech/services-and-software/its-not-that-hard-to-unmask-real-people-in-anonymous-data-researchers-warn.

40. Anne Coughlan, "New Cloud Computing Accounting Guidance" (BKD, 2018), https://www.bkd.com/sites/default/files/2018-09/New-Cloud-Computing-Accounting-Guidance.pdf.

41. Robert I. Sutton, "Memo to the CEO: Are you the source of workplace dysfunction?" (McKinsey, 2017), https://www.mckinsey.com/featured-insights/leadership/memo-to-the-ceo-are-you-the-source-of-workplace-dysfunction.

42. Served in Fleur by Hubert Keller in Las Vegas, the FleurBurger 5000 is the most expensive burger not only in the US but also in the world and comes with a price tag of US $5,000 (see "World's Most Expensive Dishes," Luxhabitat, 2019, https://www.luxhabitat.ae/the-journal/worlds-most-expensive-dish).

43. Emma Byrne, "The Science of Why Swearing Reduces Pain" (*Wired*, 2018), https://www.wired.com/story/the-science-of-why-swearing-physically-reduces-pain/.

44. Jeff Haden, "Mark Cuban Says the Best Employees Are Smart, Driven, and Curious" (*Inc. Magazine*, 2019), https://www.inc.com/jeff-haden/mark-cuban-says-best-employees-are-smart-driven-curious-but-1-skill-matters-much-more-and-makes-them-invaluable.html.

45. The Vendors in Partnership (VIP) Awards, https://www.vendorawards.com.

46. Jillian Kubala and Sade Meeks, "The 15 Best Supplements To Boost Your Immune System Right Now" (Healthline, 2021), https://www.healthline.com/nutrition/immune-boosting-supplements.

47. C. Claiborne Ray, "A Decline In The Nutritional Value Of Crops" (*New York Times*, 2015), https://www.nytimes.com/2015/09/15/science/a-decline-in-the-nutritional-value-of-crops.html.

48. Jack Garson, "Who Is Responsible When Robots Kill?" (*Forbes*, 2019), https://www.forbes.com/sites/jackgarson/2019/02/11/who-is-responsible-when-robots-kill.

49. Augie Martin, Michael Martinez, and Jason Hanna "No charges for firefighter who ran over Asiana crash survivor" (October 20, 2013), https://www.cnn.com/2013/10/18/us/asiana-firefighter-investiagtion/index.html.

50. Jakub Kaprál, "The Price Of Your Work: Here's How Much Labor Costs Around The World" (Kickresume), https://blog.kickresume.com/2019/08/13/how-much-labor-costs-around-the-world.

51. Alina Vrabie, "Productivity And Team Size: Less Is More" (Sandglaz Blog, 2013), https://blog.sandglaz.com/productivity-and-team-size-less-is-more.

52. Peter High, "After Five Years of Transformation, GM CIO Randy Mott Has the Company Primed for Innovation" (*Forbes*, 2018), https://www.forbes.com/sites/peterhigh/2018/06/18/after-five-years-of-transformation-gm-cio-randy-mott-has-the-company-primed-for-innovation/?sh=3e34604743f1.

53. "The State of the CIO in 2018" (Spencer Stuart, 2018) https://www.spencerstuart.com/research-and-insight/the-state-of-the-cio-in-2018.

54. Steve Rosenbush, "Cios, Facing Rapid Change, Tend To Be Younger, With Shorter Tenure" (Wall Street Journal, 2017), https://www.wsj.com/articles/BL-CIOB-11487.

Index